# Northamptonshire
# MURDERS

Kevin Turton

Sutton Publishing

First published in the United Kingdom in 2003 by
Sutton Publishing Limited · Phoenix Mill
Thrupp · Stroud · Gloucestershire · GL5 2BU

British Library Cataloguing in Publication Data
A catalogue record for this book is available from the British Library.

ISBN 0-7509-3329-1

Typeset in 10.5/13.5 Sabon.
Typesetting and origination by
Sutton Publishing Limited.
Printed and bound in England by
J.H. Haynes & Co. Ltd, Sparkford.

# CONTENTS

# INTRODUCTION & ACKNOWLEDGEMENTS

**MURDER** – UNLAWFUL KILLING OF HUMAN BEING WITH MALICE AFORETHOUGHT.

So says the *Concise Oxford Dictionary*, but for many it means far more than that. Murder is an odious crime. It strips those involved of the thin veneer of privacy behind which we all hide. We all live our lives in relative obscurity, careful to ensure we maintain a state of anonymity within the world at large. Only those we know and trust are allowed to have any insight into our lives and that insight is tempered by what we know of them. In turn that ensures there are areas of our lives that are intentionally withheld, guarded, forever hidden from the curious enquirer.

Murder changes this. In order to understand the rationale behind the crime we must first understand the lives of those involved. This means the victim's life must be stripped of its secrets, the veneer carefully peeled away until the true personality beneath has been revealed. This life is then offered to us all. We read of it in our newspapers, watch the reconstructions on television, follow the ensuing police investigations and suffer with the families struggling to make sense of it all. We want to know all there is to know, but we are not wholly voyeurs. We agonise over every detail of the life uncovered and are distressed by the horror of the crime. At the same time we both accept and understand the need for such public exposure, recognising that without this level of disclosure any subsequent investigation would be flawed and likely to founder on the floor of a courtroom, wrecked by good defensive argument from barristers prepared to uncover any relevant factors that have not already been unveiled.

Yet for most, despite all this, even when the culprit is caught and punished there always remains an overwhelming sense of injustice. It is impossible to quantify or attempt to rationalise the devastation caused to those whose lives are forever changed by the act of wilful murder. There is a sense of inequity that can never be erased. For those whose lives are uncovered within the pages of this book that sense of injustice and unfairness remains. The dissolution of a life through the drama of a trial long since past does not relegate the resentment felt by each and every person involved to history. If it did there would be little point in history itself. To understand the past we must understand the drama of its existence. Each and every case examined in this book tries to do just that. It does, I hope, also give an insight into the society in which these people lived, the social conditions prevalent at the time, and the manner in which the law handled those involved.

Examining the cases that aroused so much public interest, and at times hostility, has been a voyage of great discovery. Northamptonshire has a rich past and the events detailed in the following pages form a great part of it. Today we have a fascination for murder or suspicious death in much the same way as previous generations had. If we did not then there would be no crime bestseller list and none of us would be captivated by the convoluted plot lines created by authors like Patricia Cornwell or P.D. James. But in fiction it is to be remembered that none of those involved in creating the drama and tension we enjoy are real, unlike the true crimes you are about to read, where the drama was very real, the tension palpable and the outcome of any legal contest a life or death battle for at least one protagonist. There is a cutting edge to true crime that no modern crime fiction writer can ever replicate. So, be fascinated by the people, horrified by the crimes and moved by the events; but above all enjoy the read.

I should like to thank Wexford Transport Contractors and Stations UK for the loan and use of their photographs; Northamptonshire Police for giving me access to the case file for the 1952 murder at Ashton; Northamptonshire Libraries for making available several photographs from their archive collection; Peterborough Library for their assistance during research into the Ashton murder case; Mr and Mrs Cook for allowing me access to Burcote Wood Farm and staff at the Northampton Mercury Archive Collection at Northamptonshire Main Library. I have used only primary sources in the research for this book.

# 1

# THE MYSTERIOUS DEATH OF LYDIA ATLEY

## Ringstead, 1850

Richard Warren, forty-seven years old, had been a labourer all his life and most of it within the parish boundary of Ringstead village, in 1864 a small, somewhat isolated hamlet of houses on the eastern edge of Northamptonshire. On the morning of 3 February that year his employer, a Mr Peach, sent him to dig out a ditch that ran alongside the narrow lane leading to Keystone. Primarily used as a cart track for ferrying a variety of produce between the two farming communities, it had always been prone to flooding in the winter. Maintaining the ditches, an essential aid to drainage, had become a normal yearly routine, particularly on the Ringstead side. Here the field had been enclosed some ten years earlier, and a hedgerow planted along the top edge of the ditch had a tendency to clog each autumn with fallen leaves. Richard Warren had been instructed to dig out the area around the base of this hedge and widen the ditch where it was possible to do so. This he had spent much of the day attempting to do. At a little after five o'clock, just as the light began to fade and as he reached the last section to require digging out, his shovel unearthed a clean, perfectly preserved human skull.

Calling to Thomas Burnham, who had been sent to assist his efforts during the course of the afternoon, he placed it carefully on top of the grassy bank and the two men sat down to examine the find in greater detail. Warren was in no doubt the head was that of Lydia Atley; Burnham agreed, but in case they were wrong it was decided to say nothing of the discovery until they had been able to dig out more of the body on the following morning. The skull was left overnight, hidden beneath a pile of freshly cut grass, but it was not until the early afternoon of the next day that Richard Warren was able to return to complete his dig. Having been sent down to the lime kilns, which were situated just below the lane, he had been forced to confess his find in order to ensure his return. Mention of the discovery and its probable identity was sufficient to stop all other work until the entire remains had been found.

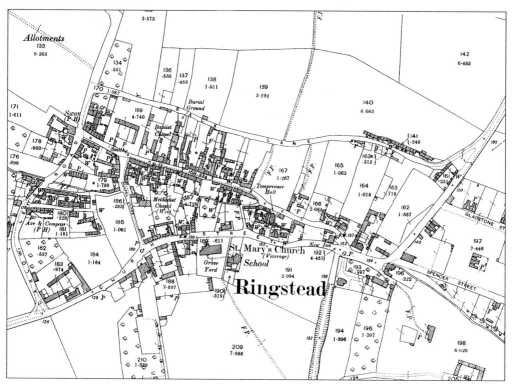

*Map of Ringstead village, c. 1850. (Northampton Library)*

By mid-afternoon Warren had uncovered the whole of the corpse. Lying face down, at right angles to the lane, head pointing to the hedgerow, feet toward the lane's centre, it was complete, but without any clothing. Police Inspector Williamson arrived just as the last shovelsful of earth were being removed. Examining the skeleton as it lay he could find no obvious cause of death, neither could he identify its sex. In his later report he stated that the body lay in a shallow grave some 18 inches deep; the ground around being dry, the bones had been well preserved. By the time Williamson had completed this cursory examination, Dr Leete, surgeon from Thrapston some two miles away, had arrived and joined him in the ditch. Under his guidance the skeleton was removed bone by bone, placed on to a wooden board, and carried to the neighbouring village of Denford less than a mile away, to an empty house owned by its vicar, a Mr Sandiland. Here Dr Leete worked late into the night trying to ascertain whether or not Richard Warren's earlier assertion had been correct. By the following morning he was able to confirm that the body had been in the ground for between twelve and twenty years and was that of a woman. Other than that, his night's work had yielded little else. So began a mystery that has endured to the present day.

Lydia Atley had been a native of Ringstead for most of her life. At the time of her disappearance some fourteen years earlier she was known to have been suffering from scurvy and to have been heavily pregnant. Police put her age at around thirty. There was no official record of her birth but the estimate was believed to be fair. For most of those thirty years she had endured grinding poverty, taking work wherever she could and peddling herrings and oranges when she could find no regular employment. In May 1850 her mother had died, heaping more despair on to an already desperate life. Lydia took the death particularly badly, forcing her older married sister, Sarah Ann, to move out of her marital home and into the house Lydia shared with her brother John. Whether Sarah's husband objected to all this sisterly love is not known but he appears not to have shouted his opposition to his neighbours too loudly. For Lydia it probably would have made little difference. Having her sister replace her mother was of paramount importance, more so since she was also pregnant – at the time of her mother's death by some seven months – and her condition was the cause of much speculation, most of it centred around Ringstead's only butcher, William Weekley Ball.

A married man with children, it was common knowledge that Ball had been seeing Lydia. Secrets are hard to keep in small villages and Ball had been seen on more than one occasion over the past year skulking around back streets and country roads pursuing his illicit affair. When Lydia became pregnant there was only one person at which to point the finger. Ball of course denied any involvement, insisting that Lydia had not been meeting him but someone else; probably, he postulated, James Wilkinson the baker and alleged father of her first child. But the locals dismissed this as nonsense; he had not appeared in Ringstead for some time they argued, neither had the two of them been sighted together. Ball on the other hand had been seen with Lydia, not just by those who had stumbled upon them in the dark either, but by her own family.

On the evening of 22 July, with most people openly speculating as to his guilt and Lydia now a full nine months into her pregnancy,

*The lane along which the first skeleton was found in 1864. (Author's Collection)*

Ball's standing within the community was at its lowest. Expected to give birth at any time, Lydia had just spent a difficult day with the younger of her two sisters, Sarah Dix, who only lived a few streets away. Sarah had been ill after a particularly difficult birth some weeks earlier and Lydia had been visiting on a fairly regular basis to help nurse her back to health. But now with her own pregnancy reaching confinement stage she had begun to find her condition restrictive. Throughout the day she had complained of feeling unwell. One of her legs had become swollen and painful, which had hampered her general movement even more. Forced to limit any amount of work or household chores to the minimum because of her physical awkwardness, her nursing usefulness had therefore become ever more ineffectual, though by this time Sarah had begun to show signs of a return to health and the daily visits had become less arduous.

At around eight-thirty that night Lydia, like many women before and since, returned to her own home with a craving for something sweet, something milky, something easy to make. She wanted a rice pudding. Older sister Sarah Ann, who had arrived to spend the night, was persuaded to walk with her to the shop to buy the necessary rice. When they got back to the house it was just after nine o'clock and because it was late into the evening Sarah suggested they should wash before they ate. Lydia said she had to go out again first, claiming there was someone she had to see, but that she would only be a short while. Fifteen minutes later she was back at her younger sister's, though for no apparent reason other than to check she was still well. After a stay of no more than half an hour she left.

At around a quarter to ten that same night, while walking back home, she met Joseph Groom, a neighbour she had known for the past sixteen years and a man she had cooked for after his first wife died. The two talked for ten minutes or so and according to his later testimony she told him she was off to see Weekley Ball to obtain some money. There was no need to ask her why; like everyone else in the village he considered the young butcher to be responsible for Lydia's pregnant state. So lighting a pipe he walked with her along the Ringstead road and left her near to the orchard behind Weekley Ball's house. A few minutes later, as he made his way back home, he clearly heard Lydia talking in a raised voice to a man he believed to be Ball. A row ensued, though much of it Joseph could not make out, and after a few minutes' loitering outside his own house alone with his pipe he gave up and returned indoors.

Elsewhere, though, this row was being clearly observed. A labourer by the name of John Hill had been walking out across the fields that fringed the village, taking advantage of the balmy night. As he wandered back along the footpath to Ringstead he had to pass along the bottom side of Weekley Ball's orchard. Suddenly aware of raised voices ahead, and not wanting to be seen, he had hidden in the hedgerow skirting the narrow path, then watched as the two met. Having known Ball for over thirty years he was certain of the

*The site of William Weekley Ball's orchard was to the left of the trees. (Author's Collection)*

man's identity and from his concealed position in the undergrowth he was well placed to hear much of what went on. According to his later story, Lydia told Ball that the baby was his, that there was no one else involved and that he should give her money. The row became heated when Ball tried to entice her to go into the orchard, which Lydia refused to do, but Ball was insistent and as she turned to walk away down the narrow lane into the village he took hold of her. At that point the rowing ceased. Hill heard the latch of the gate to the orchard being lifted and as he peered through the dense foliage of the hedge he watched as the two disappeared among the trees. No more was ever seen of Lydia Atley.

Within days of her disappearance William Weekley Ball was arrested on a charge of murder and arraigned before Thrapston magistrates, but the case was thrown out of court after diligent searching failed to discover a body. However, ostracised by his neighbours and boycotted by his customers, he was forced to leave Ringstead. Moving into Cambridgeshire he opened a new business in the then small village of Ramsey, and there he would no doubt have stayed had Richard Warren never cleared that ditch alongside the narrow lane to Keystone fourteen years later.

Once the skeleton had been examined and clearly identified as being female, Weekley Ball was arrested for the second time and brought to Thrapston. Committal proceedings began on 26 February 1864 before General Arburthnot, and the courthouse was packed to capacity. Outside, and spilling into the street, a crowd unable to gain admittance gathered in the hope of catching just a glimpse of Ball as he arrived, so intense was the interest from surrounding villages – though according to press reports at the time, most who gathered were certain of his guilt. Indeed, Ball would have struggled to find any who held a contrary view. For those who stood in the cold that day, justice had at long last caught up with the Ringstead butcher.

By the time of the committal hearings Ball was described by the *Northampton Mercury* as being between forty and fifty years old:

[He] was dressed very respectfully in black, and had the appearance of a well to do tradesman. He has a rather high, bald forehead, with a single lock of long dark hair drawn across it, a well-shaped nose, thin lips, and eyes with many wrinkles about them. The face is peculiar from a complete absence of eyebrows.

Being of such good social standing had, from a financial point of view at any rate, allowed Ball to pay to secure a legal defence. A Mr Gaches, solicitor of Peterborough, had been hired to take on the role and this he did with great conviction. After hearing initial witness evidence from Lydia's sisters and key testimony from Joseph Groom and John Hill, all of which proved mainly circumstantial, it was the turn of the medical men. If guilt was to be proved they had to show that the skeleton was that of Lydia Atley. This was no simple task and Mr Gaches knew it. He also knew that the only piece of

*Thrapston Courthouse, 2003. (Author's Collection)*

identification evidence possessed by the prosecution came from a villager named Henry Dix (brother-in-law to younger sister Sarah). Two weeks prior to her disappearance Lydia had suffered an excruciating toothache. Unable to pay for its extraction she had asked Dix to pull the offending tooth out. This he had only agreed to do after a prolonged debate about the state of her health. According to his testimony the tooth in question had been on the left side of her lower jaw, third tooth counted from the back and he had used a pair of pincers to remove it. Having been allowed to examine the unearthed skull he had been able to confirm that it too was missing a tooth in exactly the same place. Two doctors, Mr Leete of Thrapston and Mr William Orlando Markham of St Mary's Hospital, London, offered corroborating post-mortem evidence that supported his argument. The skull, minus several teeth, showed clear evidence of only one of these missing teeth being lost through extraction and that, in their estimation, shortly before death. By the end of the first day it was looking decidedly bleak for Weekley Ball.

No doubt there was much discussion between Mr Gaches and his client after the day's events, with the solicitor reassuring Weekley Ball over the conjectural nature of much of what had been heard. Certainly when Ball reappeared for Saturday's committal resumption he showed no outward signs of concern, the *Northampton Mercury* reporting that 'he showed not the least agitation'. As the day's proceedings continued with medical testimony, perhaps he felt on safe ground.

Having discussed at some length the issue of the missing tooth in this opening session, the court turned its attention to that of identification. There was no doubt the skeleton found was that of a woman, but was that woman Lydia Atley? Mr Gaches was convinced that it was not. From the day's opening exchanges it became clear he had every intention of proving his point. Dr Leete had been brought back to the stand to complete his previous day's testimony, none of which proved particularly contentious, that is until he concluded his findings as to the skeleton's sex. Aware that enough gender evidence existed, Mr Gaches knew there was little point to further argument. He also knew, however, as did the whole court, that at the time of her supposed death Lydia Atley was nine months pregnant. To where, he asked, had the unborn child disappeared?

Mr Gaches: If this is the skeleton of a woman, and she was 9 months with child, as Lydia Atley was said to have been, ought you not to have found some foetal remains?

Doctor Leete: There is a probability that there would have been some.

Gaches had sowed serious doubt. The first flaw in the prosecution had been brought to the surface and he rammed home his point. Calling William

*Back Lane, Ringstead, Lydia lived nearby and the two often met near here. (Author's Collection)*

Orlando Markham back to the stand Gaches asked the same question, to which he received a similar reply. For the first time in two days there was real hope. But it was not to last.

As the day drew towards a close the prosecution launched its last and most devastating piece of evidence. It appeared that shortly after Lydia's disappearance William Weekley Ball had travelled to Northampton to meet a man he had known for some years; furthermore, a man he believed would not be averse to a little subterfuge. The man was William Weekley (no relation) and what he asked him to do was to write a letter. But this was to be no ordinary letter. Knowing that William's mother lived in Ringstead he wanted a letter to say that Lydia Atley had been seen, alive and well, in Northampton. For whatever reason William agreed to the suggestion:

> . . . I recollect the prisoner [Weekley Ball] coming to me about a fortnight or three weeks after Lydia Atley was missed and his saying he wanted to speak to me. We then went to the Ram Inn together and sat in a long room. There was no other person in the room. He then told me that he wanted me to write a letter to say I had seen Lydia Atley. I knew the woman, but I had not seen her for five weeks previous to this time, as I had been in Northampton about six weeks. I wrote a letter, and I sent it to my mother by post. I posted it myself. In this letter I enclosed a note for the prisoner, and wrote, 'Give this to Weekley.'

*Ringstead church where the 1906 skeleton was buried. (Author's Collection)*

It was damning stuff, but at the conclusion of this evidence from William Weekley it transpired that the letter he talked of could not be produced in its original format. Eliza Weekley, the letter's recipient, had done exactly as her son had asked and passed it to Weekley Ball without understanding its content or meaning. Reading ability in 1850 was not at its strongest. He in turn had offered it to the police during their questioning of him fourteen years earlier and then destroyed it. Unfortunately for the defence the police officer who met Ball all those years ago had copied the letter, which had been retrieved from old police records:

Northampton August 12th 1850.

I write you a few lines to inform you that I saw L. Atley in Northampton. I was going down Castle Street, at about eight p.m., or half past eight p.m., on Sunday night. There was a man with her with a long smock frock on, and a cape.

William Weekley.

There was no going back. The court found the defendant guilty of murder and committed him for trial at the next Northampton Assizes. The only voice offered up in his defence was that of the *Northampton Mercury*. In its

*Thrapston road leading to Denford. The skeleton believed to be Lydia Atley discovered in 1906 was found somewhere along this road. (Author's Collection)*

editorial of 5 March 1864 it contested that the crux of any successful prosecution must lie in the proving of three issues. One, that Lydia Atley was ever murdered. Two, that the skeleton found was hers, and thirdly that Weekley Ball was her murderer. In its opinion, it argued, the Thrapston court had failed to prove any of the issues sufficiently enough to warrant an eventual verdict that would send him to the gallows. It was a lone voice; most of Northamptonshire had no such doubts.

The editorial, however, proved both fortuitous and perceptive when later that same day a second skeleton was unearthed within yards of the first, this time that of a man. Examination showed that it could have been buried at around the same time as the woman's and was believed to have been that of a gypsy. As a result it cast sufficient doubt on the case against William Weekley Ball and there was little choice other than to release him without further charge. It made little difference to those who knew him, though; his guilt was still widely accepted and his business in Ramsey was subsequently ruined. Towards the end of the 1860s he returned to live in Ringstead, possibly hoping he would fare better among a community he knew despite their misgivings over his culpability. He died there in 1890.

At that point the story of the disappearance or murder of Lydia Atley ought to have ended, but in 1906 while further work was being carried out in the same area another body was found. This time it was more easily confirmed as being that of a woman, about thirty years of age and lying beside a rusted, open, cut-throat razor. . . .

Lydia Atley?

# 2

# A DEADLY INHERITANCE

*Daventry, 1851*

Francis Mutton had lived a rich and comfortable life, accruing wealth and property. Unfortunately, at the time of his death he had no children to inherit it, so while lying on his deathbed he wrote a will expressing his wish that everything must be sold and the proceeds of that sale given to his niece, Elizabeth Pinckard, a woman who, by then, was well past the age of seventy. A sum of £1,000 was duly raised which would no doubt have changed the life of struggle she and her husband Richard had endured for years, had she been able to access the capital sum. Sadly for the two of them, her uncle had added a provisory clause to his will preventing her from doing just that. Instead she was to be paid only the interest this sum accrued while invested in a trust fund. The fund itself was to be dissolved only upon her own death, at which point its full value was to be paid to her son John.

With this knowledge in mind John, who had little by way of business acumen, took possession of a farm known locally as Thrupp grounds. A tenant farmer, he maintained a small dairy herd and farmed a number of acres of prime agricultural land. Together with his wife they fostered a belief among the local community that theirs was a comfortable lifestyle, that the farm was flourishing and that they had sufficient capital to ensure its continued growth. A local girl was employed as housemaid and a number of men were retained as general hands about the farm. As far as most were concerned John and his wife had a tight rein on those twin attributes that guarantee success: affluence and influence. Few would have challenged their growing status within the community, or so it seemed.

But by the end of September 1851 a small group of businessmen had begun to realise that all was not well at the farm at Thrupp grounds. Thomas Wathorne, who owned the farmhouse and its land and had not been paid rent for a number of months, expressed a concern about the viability of John Pinckard's farm. His was not a lone voice; others too had shared suspicions and were beginning to voice them, albeit at that stage only among themselves. Nevertheless it was a worsening situation and one the Pinckards knew they must address if they were to maintain their carefully cultivated status. So, no doubt viewing their landlord as the man with the loudest voice and the greatest influence, they set up a meeting at the beginning of October. It did not go well. John Pinckard had hoped to be able to extend his credit, possibly into the New Year, but Wathorne was unrelenting. He insisted they borrow money to pay off their debts, using the future £1,000 inheritance as collateral. Refusal as far as he was concerned meant eviction. Borrowing was the last thing either of the Pinckards wanted to do, particularly against their eventual legacy. Interest charges over a number of untold years could destroy the lump sum even before they managed to get their hands on it if they were not careful; to John there seemed little choice, not so his wife.

On the morning of Friday 3 October, John's wife, Elizabeth, who shared a common name with her mother-in-law but little else, left the farm at around ten o'clock in the morning. Thomas Hadland, who they had employed to thatch the barn roof, watched her from his lofty vantage point as she made her way across the fields toward Daventry. Once out of sight of the farmhouse she clambered through the hedgerow and on to the Long Buckby road, where some hundred or so yards ahead of her lay the cottage home of John's parents. But this was to be no social call. Elizabeth knew that her father-in-law had left to go to Daventry agricultural fair earlier that morning. He and her husband had taken a horse they hoped to sell. In fact, knowing this had given her the courage to make the walk that particular morning; had the fair not been that week she would probably never have left the house. But it seemed too good an opportunity to miss. Standing on the brink of bankruptcy Elizabeth had determined to resolve their financial plight once and for all. As she entered the back door of the old cottage that morning the only obstacle to certain security stood before the kitchen sink – her mother-in-law.

*The Long Buckby road looking toward Daventry. (Author's Collection)*

The old woman had been doing a little sewing; a bag containing various bits of cotton, cloth and dressmaker's tape sat open on the kitchen table. It was the tape that caught Elizabeth's eye the moment she entered the house. Distracting her mother-in-law for a moment she lifted it from the sewing bag, made a slip knot, put it over her mother-in-law's head and pulled tightly. There was a struggle, of sorts, but the younger woman's greater strength quickly prevailed and the old woman soon slumped to the floor, dead. Leaving her where she lay, Elizabeth took the tape – a length of some two yards – and with the ligature still in place around the dead woman's neck searched out a hook high up on the wall beside her. She wanted the world at large to believe it had been suicide, that the old woman had hanged herself from the hook that had once been used to hang fresh game. But there was a problem; with the body in a prone position the tape was too short. It took a good few minutes to lift her mother-in-law into a sitting position, but once done enough tape was freed and Elizabeth was just able to make it stretch. Satisfied the scene looked as she intended, she left. The time was half past eleven. Thomas Hadland, still thatching, watched her return to the farm some fifteen minutes later and quite probably Elizabeth believed she had just committed the perfect murder.

At around half past five that evening Thomas Bird, who rented a field adjacent to the cottage on the Long Buckby road, released his pony into the little paddock, after which he walked to the back of the house and entered through the open door. Old Mrs Pinckard still sat where Elizabeth had left her; no one else had been into the house. Shocked, but realising almost immediately that she was dead, he cut down the tape, then leaving her still in a sitting position, he ran out into the street shouting 'Murder!' Within a quarter of an hour Dr Sharman, Daventry's surgeon, had arrived on the scene and after a cursory examination told the waiting crowd of neighbours that she had probably committed suicide. It was a further hour before her husband was found and told.

There the case would have ended, consigned to history and obscurity, had it not been for two significant factors: one, that Elizabeth Pinckard had been seen making the call on her mother-in-law; and two, that Dr Sharman found blood. In the case of the first it transpired that when Elizabeth arrived at the cottage that morning she was seen by two men who were working on the road some hundred yards or so away. One of these men, John Letts, also saw her leave. Furthermore, the local beat bobby, William Reynolds, had seen her just inside the open door of the cottage as he walked past on his normal daily route around the village. This did not seem important until, when told of the death, Elizabeth Pinckard, apparently confident no one had seen her, claimed that she had not been to her mother-in-law's cottage for over a week. But perhaps more significant was the doctor's discovery of a smudged bloodstain on the kitchen wall to the left of the body. Closer examination of the body

*Daventry's Moot Hall, c. 1900. (Northampton Library)*

showed a head wound, a cut above the left eye, not at first clearly discernible but a wound that had bled. The doctor at first took the view that the old woman had struggled violently after trying to launch herself off into eternity, that as a result her head had struck the wall, caused the cut and left the blood mark. Only after carefully checking out the scene did he begin to change that opinion. The blood was a smudged stain, as if a hand had brushed against it, and to hang from the hook in the manner she had been found precluded any possibility that she could have struck the wall during her death throes. It was too far away. He decided that it could only be as found if the old woman had been murdered. Elizabeth Pinckard, despite strenuous denials, was arrested on Monday 6 October and charged with the killing.

On that same day the inquest opened at the Boot Inn, Daventry, presided over by Mr P.E. Hicks who, concerned by the large crowd that tried to force its way into the only room available, promptly had it adjourned and moved to the Moot Hall where facilities were better. It was a short affair, hearing evidence through the course of the afternoon, which showed that only Elizabeth Pinckard had any opportunity that day to have carried out a murder. The two workmen insisted they had stayed on the road from early morning until the discovery of the body late that same day. It was all the coroner's jury needed and after a half-hour consultation they returned a unanimous verdict of wilful murder against her.

For the next four months Elizabeth Pinckard languished in a cell in Northampton prison, never changing her plea of innocence and insisting throughout that some passing tramp or traveller had murdered her mother-in-law. When she came to trial on 27 February 1852 the court was besieged by crowds who had travelled in from all parts of Northamptonshire, all eager to hear if this claim of innocence would be borne out by the facts. Rumour and speculation had spread throughout much of the county, fanned by reports from the prison that she had resisted all attempts to change her plea. It therefore took some time for Judge Jervis to bring order to his court when he took his seat at ten o'clock that morning, and allow the trial to begin.

From the outset there was to be little succour for the woman in the dock. During those intervening months no one had been found who could substantiate anything she had offered up in her own defence. Only a line of witnesses, ushered in one after the other, all of whom testified to having seen her during the key hours of the morning in question. The perfect murder Elizabeth thought she had committed had been nothing but a

*Daventry town, 2003. (Author's Collection)*

complete shambles. But stoically she stuck to the story she had first told police when they arrested her, that she had been away from the house during the morning to gather blackberries, that she had eaten all she gathered and that shortly after her return to the farmhouse she had torn her dress on the key to the dairy door. Of course it was never believed, but she knew that while it may be shown she had gone to the cottage, no one could prove she had committed the murder. What Elizabeth had not considered, however, was the testimony of her own maidservant and how damaging it would be.

Ann Cross did most of the household chores. On the morning of the murder she was in the house when Elizabeth returned, and remarked upon the torn dress, believing it would be assigned to her to do the necessary repairs. But later that same afternoon she had been pleasantly surprised to find Elizabeth doing her own sewing, and even more so when later she found the dress had been washed out twice. According to the maid's evidence Elizabeth Pinckard never washed any clothing, so to find that this particular dress had been given such royal treatment was incomprehensible; there had to be a reason. While Ann had no idea what this was, the police investigating the murder certainly did.

Dr Sharman had told the inquest at Daventry, and reiterated his evidence in Northampton, that there had been blood found on the kitchen wall. Further blood spots had been discovered later on the floor and around the doorway. When Edward Osborne, the Daventry police officer responsible for the arrest, had searched the Pinckards' farmhouse he had found blood on two different garments, an apron and a shawl. The prosecution's contention was that the blood found on the shawl had come from Elizabeth's mother-in-law during the struggle to kill her. Every witness brought to court that day had sworn to having seen Elizabeth either wearing or carrying a shawl, and while positive identification of the shawl in question could not be made, it fitted the general description for type and colour. Furthermore, they contested, if blood had been found on this, and had also been spread around the house, then it seemed highly likely that whatever dress had been worn would have been likewise stained. This, they went on, was why it had been washed twice and why it could not be left out for the maid to take care of. Elizabeth Pinckard knew the police would come knocking; if they found any blood on her dress she would have been damned. It was a powerful argument and one that the jury were content to accept. It took only fifteen minutes to return a guilty verdict.

It had been common practice to execute convicted prisoners two weeks after their sentencing and normally on a Friday. In previous years the prison authorities had posted details of coming executions in order to ensure a large crowd to what was a public spectacle. But by 1852 this practice was in decline. Authorities no longer posted details of impending executions, and although still carried out in public, the timing was generally kept secret. In the case of Elizabeth Pinckard the populace at large believed her public hanging would take place on 12 March. As a result, and believing the timing had been deliberately withheld, they descended upon Northampton in their thousands. They came from all walks of life, from the lowest to the highest, many arriving with children in tow, others with food parcels and, according to the *Northampton Mercury*, the vast majority were women. Whatever their reasons for attending, they were disappointed. No execution took place that day and the crowd began to disperse by mid-afternoon, satisfied they would miss nothing by leaving, and sure in the knowledge they would be back.

While all this was going on outside the prison, inside it a petition was being mounted with the hope of gaining a reprieve. A flurry of activity led by numerous legal notaries had resulted in a document being drawn up calling for a reduction of sentence from that of murder to one of manslaughter. At the time there was a strong belief among those instigating it that it ought to meet with success. There was a precedent – women were rarely executed; the courts would generally find in their favour by one means or another. In the case of Elizabeth Pinckard, however, they were less inclined to view her crime with a lenient eye. The Home Secretary rejected the plea on 14 March.

On 15 March, twenty-four hours before her execution, Elizabeth Pinckard met the prison chaplain, Thomas Hutton. It was a short but highly emotional meeting during which she explained, for the first time, just what had happened on that day back in October 1851:

> I went to the cottage on purpose to do it. I took the tape out of the bag which was open on the table, when she was fumbling among the flowerpots in the window. I made a slip knot with the tape doubled, put it over her head, and drew it quite tight. She shook her head several times from side to side, and then shuddered down in the corner. I afterwards fastened the tape to the hook and then left her. I did nothing to her dress, or her hands, but as she sliddered down, so I left her. I did not snatch the tape but drew it tightly, and held it firmly. She threw her head from side to side a good deal, and perhaps she then gave herself the blow on the eye against the edge of the wall. I do not know that there was any blood from the wound. I did not see any. My husband is as innocent of this matter as a child unborn and I trust to God that his character will never be blasted on account of my guilt.

The following day at eight o'clock in the morning, possibly buoyed up by this confession, Elizabeth Pinckard made the short walk to the scaffold without the attendance of a huge crowd and paid the ultimate penalty for her greed. A few days earlier her husband John had received a gift of £1,000 from his murdered mother's estate.

# 3

# FOR THE SAKE OF FOURTEEN SHILLINGS

*Rothwell, 1855*

Isaac Pinnock was described as being an unfortunate man. Physically handicapped since birth, he had been unable to work for any of his nineteen years. Relying upon his father to provide for him, he had developed no skills that would have enabled him to be self-sufficient. He had been shunned by much of the local community, among whom he was known to be a wastrel, no doubt owing to his total disregard for their property over the years: Pinnock had little compunction when it came to robbery. So he grew up with himself for company and without much in the way of education. His right leg dragged behind him when he walked which necessitated the use of a stick, so there was no disguising his presence wherever he went; and he spent his days wandering aimlessly around the footpaths and open countryside of Rothwell. By the summer of 1855 he had become a familiar, if somewhat unwelcome, figure.

Benjamin Cheney, on the other hand, had a reputation and a position in life that most would have envied. Farmer, businessman and much respected citizen, he had evolved a lifestyle far removed from that of Isaac Pinnock. Born in 1775, he spent his growing years in a more privileged household. Educationally equipped for an advantaged life, it is probably fair to say that he had lived well for most of his eighty years. There was, therefore, no reason for these two men to ever meet, other than in passing through the town, had not Isaac Pinnock engineered it through a series of bungled attempts at robbery. For much of 1855, mainly through mischief or sheer vandalism, Pinnock had either been seen or found attempting to force locks from Cheney's barns and outbuildings. No serious lasting damage had been caused and nothing had been stolen, that is until the end of June that year. Aware that Cheney had locked a ewe and her newly born lamb into a barn, Pinnock had successfully forced his way in and stolen away with them both, though what he intended to do with the sheep when he had no means to keep them himself, and slaughter was impractical, was never established. Benjamin Cheney found all three of them, within hours, hidden inside an old, ramshackle hovel not far from his farm. The ewe died within twenty-four

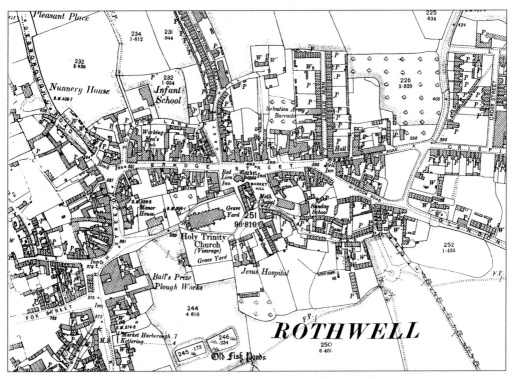

*Map of Rothwell, 1900. The footpath used by Benjamin Cheney is shown toward the bottom of the map. (Northampton Library)*

hours and days later, when the two men met again on Rothwell High Street, Cheney threatened Pinnock publicly with prison if he ever found him on his property again. It was a threat he would regret.

On 6 July, two weeks after the incident, Benjamin Cheney set out to walk the four or five miles from his Rothwell home to Kettering market. Armed with 14s in silver, 6d in ha'pennies and a cheque drawn for £20, he intended to do business with local traders, possibly for livestock. It had become a normal routine. His was a familiar face among those buying and selling and most knew his preferred route along the footpaths that ran between the two small townships. At a little after a quarter past twelve he was seen crossing what were known locally as the Slates, the first of several fields he had to cross along the Kettering footpath. The name, derived from a local farmer, Slate, who once owned the land, and sometimes known as Slate's Piece, was a long narrow field that in 1855 marked a divide between two farms owned by a Mr Shortland and a Mr Beeby. By twelve-thirty Cheney had left this field behind and was on the Kettering side of a narrow brook that dissected the land. This was seen as a boundary line by most locals and a number of wooden planks had been laid across to form a narrow bridge. Just beyond stood a stile, and a mile or so further on were the outskirts of Kettering. But Benjamin Cheney never reached his market destination. At a little before one o'clock in the afternoon Rhoda Tye and her daughter Sarah found his body on the Kettering side of the stile. He had been bludgeoned to death with what appeared to Rhoda to have been something with a sharp cutting edge.

Leaving her daughter to mount guard, Rhoda Tye ran into Rothwell and brought back Patrick M'Loskey, surgeon, to confirm her first impression. There was no doubt. The man had received one blow to the top of the head, which in the doctor's opinion would have stunned him, and a single blow to the back of the head, shattering the skull and exposing the brain. This second blow, the doctor hypothesised, would have brought death almost instantaneously. As far as he was able to tell after such a cursory examination, the weapon used had to have been a small, sharp axe – a common enough tool in a farming community. The body was then removed and carried to the Bell Inn, Rothwell, where further examination of his clothing revealed that none of the ha'pennies remained in his trouser pockets, only the £20 cheque, and all the silver was missing. Robbery formed the instant and obvious motive.

While all this was taking place Police Inspector Keep had arrived at the scene and was examining the ground where the body had been discovered. The weather had been dry for days and footprints were clearly discernible in the dust, in particular one set that showed their owner had a very distinct handicap. Whoever had been around that stile during the course of that day, apart from Benjamin Cheney, had a right foot that dragged along the ground and had made use of a walking stick. The distinctive markings were there for all to see. After retracing these footsteps back to the narrow brook, some 15 yards away from the murder scene, the inspector found a short axe, carelessly discarded, its head and wooden shaft still red with blood, its cutting edge covered in hair that matched Benjamin Cheney's. It was not difficult to deduce that the owner of the footprints and the man who had wielded the axe were one and the same.

Inspector Keep was knocking at the door of John Pinnock, Isaac's father, within the hour. After a rudimentary search of both the house and its outbuildings he found a matching axe to the one he had discovered at the murder site. It lay where it had been discarded days earlier after being used to cut back hedgerows. John Pinnock told the inspector that it was one of a matching pair and after being shown the axe that had killed Benjamin Cheney he identified the second axe as his own. Minutes later Isaac Pinnock was in custody. From the outset it seemed a clear-cut case. Isaac had obviously been at the stile where the body had been found and had easy access to the weapon used in the killing. What could he possibly offer in his defence? But Isaac was not about to roll over and admit guilt. He insisted he had not committed any murder, had not been in the area of the Kettering footpath and had not carried out any robbery. Examination of all his clothing showed no bloodstaining and, furthermore, no money had been found either on his

*The footpath as it looks in 2003. (Author's Collection)*

person or at his father's house. Despite all this, when Mr William Marshall opened the inquest at Rothwell's Bell Inn on the following day, 7 July, Isaac Pinnock was the only suspect in custody.

However, the police had certainly been diligent in their investigation over the previous twenty-four hours in questioning a number of key witnesses, all of whom were in a position to discredit much of Isaac Pinnock's denial. After listening to evidence of identity and corroborating evidence from Cheney's housemaid, Elizabeth Kilsby, with regard to the amount of money Cheney was carrying when he set out to Kettering market, the first of these key witnesses took the stand at the committal hearing. Charles Morris, labourer, told the court that Pinnock had been standing beside the stile where the murder took place at eleven-thirty that morning. The two men had passed each other without speaking. Further corroboration came from Rothwell's baker, John Botterill. He had crossed the same stile at around midday. The two had exchanged a few words. Botterill told the court of his surprise at having found Isaac so far from his home when, in his opinion, walking that distance with such a handicap must have been both tiring and difficult. Isaac had apparently been very reticent, loitering around the hedgerow that grew either side of the stile, preferring silence to conversation. But the most damning piece of testimony came from Mr Taylor, the farmer responsible at that time for managing Slate's Piece. He had been out riding his land during the course of the morning, at about eighteen minutes to one – and here he was very precise – when he saw Isaac making his way along the hedgerow that skirted the field's boundary from the stile along the footpath, to the place he sat astride his horse. Shouting at him to get out of the field, that he was trespassing, Taylor watched him until satisfied he was doing nothing wrong, then rode away.

*Glendon Road looking toward Rothwell with the Bell Inn shown in the distance. The footpath lay just beyond the last house. (Author's Collection)*

It may have all been circumstantial but it was enough for the jury who, after a fairly lengthy deliberation, considered Isaac Pinnock guilty of murder and sent him for trial.

A week later he stood in the dock at Northampton's courthouse and pleaded not guilty. Counsel was appointed for him and the trial began at ten o'clock in the morning. Having had a further two weeks or so to examine the body of the murdered man, Doctor Patrick M'Loskey was now able to be more specific as to the wounds sustained by Benjamin Cheney and from which direction they had been inflicted. Thorough post-mortem examination had confirmed his earlier, somewhat hurried diagnosis, that two distinct blows to the head had been made by an axe. The smaller injury of the two was responsible for knocking the man down, the second wound, some four inches long, was responsible for his death. This second blow had been delivered with some force and had penetrated the brain by just over an inch. In his opinion Benjamin Cheney had been taken completely by surprise and struck from the back, just to his left side, consistent with having just made as if to mount the first step of the stile, beneath which his body had been found.

The court-appointed defence counsel, Mr O'Brien, was instantly on his feet to claim that the blow, had it been delivered as the good doctor suggested, must have been made by the left hand. The doctor agreed. Isaac Pinnock was right-handed. The first hole in the prosecution case appeared to have been

*The Bell Inn, now renamed The Pub. (Author's Collection)*

made. But there were to be no further gains. After listening to a variety of witness evidence, none of which was contested and all of which placed Isaac at the scene, it appeared, as at the inquest, that little by way of defence could be argued. The morning slowly slipped away and as the last witness left the stand, after offering a damning assessment of the footprints found around the body and their probable owner, nothing had been uncovered or revealed to prove either probity or mitigation beyond the slim piece of speculative medical evidence heard at the outset of the case.

So, when Mr O'Brien took to his feet at the closing of the trial it was almost certainly to defend a lost cause. Sufficient evidence had been heard by this time to place the rope around Isaac Pinnock's neck and publicly hang him. But the defence speech, when it came, was powerful and persuasive. O'Brien argued strongly that to assert, as the prosecution had through the numerous witnesses produced, that Pinnock had been loitering to murderous intent on the day of the murder, that his footprints around the scene confirmed his involvement and that because the axe came from his father's barn his was the hand that wielded it was, he insisted, pure conjecture. As a handicapped man, he contended, whose clubbed-foot disability rendered employment impossible, murder in such a manner could not be countenanced, and loitering about the town and countryside was all Pinnock could ever do:

He was seen loitering about on a market day in a public footway; but they must remember that an unfortunate cripple like him was necessarily always loitering about. He was unable to work; he had no amusement at home, and he could only seek amusement in the open air watching the people pass to and fro. . . . The footprints, supposing them to be his, were entirely consistent with his innocence. Grant that he had made that track, what evidence was there that it had not been made hours or even days before the murder. . . . The unfortunate prisoner, on whom the hand of affliction seemed to have fallen heavily from his birth was charged with an offence which, crippled as he was, it seemed most impossible for him to have committed.

It was a valid argument. The whole case had been mounted upon the back of circumstantial evidence. Nothing had ever been found to prove beyond doubt that the man in the dock had actually stolen, let alone wielded, the axe. Even the contentious issue of the footprints, which from the outset had appeared insurmountable, Mr O'Brien did his utmost to discredit. Furthermore, as he reminded the jury, Isaac Pinnock had been arrested within two hours of the body's discovery without any incriminating evidence being found on his person:

> . . . no trace of the silver or copper, which it was certain had been taken from the pockets of the murdered man, were to be found. Then, too, the dress of the prisoner had not a spot of blood upon it, although the axe was covered with blood, and the case for the prosecution went upon the supposition that he had carried it a considerable distance.

Again O'Brien scored a valid point, but the judge was not about to allow the jury to retire and form a verdict built solely around this defence argument. He instructed that though the evidence was circumstantial and warranted circumspection they must not mistake timidity for caution. It took no more than half an hour for the jury to show they had not. Isaac Pinnock was duly sentenced to death.

The conviction brought about a flurry of protest, most of it through letters to the editor of the *Northampton Mercury*. Immediately the verdict was returned the newspaper had taken the stance that it would not support a public execution. Its editorials argued strongly against such an action, believing such a penalty flew in the face of public decency and against the Christian principles most people upheld. It was a view that began to find support among its readership, though it has to be remembered that a large portion of the Northamptonshire population had few reading skills.

As the debate raged, presumably without Isaac Pinnock's knowledge, he made an unexpected and unlooked-for confession. Within days of his conviction news was beginning to surface that during a private meeting with the prison chaplain he had sought absolution, that as a prerequisite of that absolution he had been required to acknowledge his involvement in the murder. This apparently Isaac had freely done, informing the police that on the morning Benjamin Cheney had set out to walk to Kettering he had resolved to kill him and steal whatever money he carried. Knowing it was the man's usual habit to attend Kettering market and knowing his preferred route, Isaac had laid in wait for him behind the first stile marking the entrance to Slate's Piece, not the second one beyond the brook and where he had been found. Unfortunately, because Cheney was later than usual Isaac had fallen asleep beneath the hedge and only awoke as his intended victim passed by. Realising opportunity was about to disappear he had grasped the axe, stolen earlier in the day, and then chased after him, only catching him at the second stile. After the killing he had taken most of the coin and buried it for later retrieval. Police subsequently recovered all the money from a hole in the ground yards from the footpath.

Execution was set for 27 July 1855, a Friday, the usual day for Northampton's convicted murderers to mount the scaffold. Fortunately for Pinnock an examination carried out two days before he was to die found he was insane, resulting in an unexpected Home Office reprieve being received just two hours before the trapdoor was to have opened beneath his feet.

# 4

# THE PRICE OF AN ARGUMENT

## *Holcot, 1871*

Holcot today is a picturesque village four or five miles north of Northampton town, its farms, cottages and barns built around a network of narrow roads. Most are built from local yellow sandstone that has matured with age and all within the lee of its church, which dominates the high ground to the west. In 1871 it was very much a farming community with most of its available labour working on the land, though not all. As the shoe industry developed throughout Northamptonshire so did the need for men and women who could work from home. This in turn had led to a growing number of households where shoe manufacture had replaced some of the more traditional home-based industrial skills. Holcot village, like many others around it, had by this time already developed a thriving community of shoemakers, mainly men, who were employed in this fashion working from their own front rooms.

Richard Addington, a native of the village, became one of this group when he returned to his birthplace in the mid-1860s, though the opportunity to return after a number of years spent in Northampton had been quite fortuitous. If it had not been for one of his two brothers writing to inform him of an imminent house build it is doubtful he would ever have returned. But the houses, once completed, were perfect for the type of work Richard had become skilled in producing. A short terrace of four two-storey houses, built on rising ground above the village pond, their only doors opened on to a square courtyard along the edge of which lay a row of outhouses and outbuildings which could be used for storage. Addington and his wife Mary lost no time in abandoning town for village, and by 1871 had become well established among the local community, Mary having given birth to three children in the intervening years, though only two, both daughters, had survived.

Outwardly theirs was a happy marriage, though there had been the odd violent outburst, particularly if Richard had been drinking. So those who knew him guarded against it, taking great pains to ensure he rarely

*Holcot old village. (Northampton Library)*

overstepped the mark. It seemed to work and the incidents of violence that had marred their relationship when living in Northampton slowly disappeared, until most would never have believed they had ever happened at all. All, that is, except Mary.

On the evening of Monday 29 May 1871 Richard had been drinking in the Chequers public house, though, as many testified later, not to excess. He was, according to those who had seen him, sober when he left the bar to walk the short distance home. Later that night, at around midnight, shouting could be heard coming from their house. It continued for some time but no neighbour reported hearing any sound of physical abuse and as it subsided after half an hour or so, no one took any further notice. Certainly by half past seven the next morning when Richard Addington walked out of his back door to cross the courtyard to talk to a neighbour it had been forgotten. At that time he appeared quite calm and rational. A couple of hours later, around ten o'clock, he and Mary were seen talking down by the duck pond, not apparently animated or angry but seemingly quite content with each other. Nothing in the demeanour of either suggested the violence that was about to happen.

Fifteen minutes after this apparently blissful scene, and after they had returned to the courtyard, Mary was heard to refuse to go back into the house. Richard made no attempt at persuasion but simply swept her up in his

*The row of cottages where Richard and Mary Addington lived. (Author's Collection)*

arms, carried her into the house and slammed the door behind them. This was followed almost immediately by her desperate screams, the door was thrown open and she staggered back into the courtyard screaming she had been murdered.

Elizabeth Warren, who had moved into her sister's house at the end of the terrace row just three days earlier, was the first neighbour to react. Mary, only able to stagger a few steps, had made straight for her door. As Elizabeth stepped out into the yard it was to find Mary on her doorstep, a hand clutching her throat but still able to speak. Propping her up against the doorjamb she tried to see past the blood, which by this time was flowing between Mary's fingers and soaking the front of her dress. Elizabeth decided the wound was deep but not life threatening if she could get medical help quickly enough. But before she had time to rouse the rest of the neighbourhood to help she was joined by Richard Addington who had followed his wife out into the courtyard. Now full of remorse he took a hold of Mary while Elizabeth continued her brief examination, then helped to carry his wife into the Warrens' kitchen. As they laid her on the floor Elizabeth tried to tell him that the wound could be treated, that it did not

*The duck pond where Mary Addington went on the morning of her murder. (Author's Collection)*

appear as serious as it looked. But words of consolation were not what Richard sought. Knowingly, he took hold of her hand and pushed it down into his wife's abdomen, saying 'that ain't the worst – there's the worst'.

Elizabeth understood the minute her hand felt the holes in Mary's dress. There was a greater blood loss from the wounds her fingers found than the single stab wound to her neck. There would be no saving the woman and as the neighbour knelt on the floor trying to stem the blood flow all three of them knew it. Stoically, Mary turned her face to her husband and calmly told him he had killed her, that her death was inevitable. He, by now in tears, acknowledged her pronouncement, telling her time was short, that she would die within minutes but that he would join her in a few hours. Without rancour or bitterness she accepted her situation, taking a reassuring hold of her husband's hand and when he repeated his request for forgiveness she granted it unconditionally.

Accepting his remorse Elizabeth Warren decided it was safe to leave the two of them together and ran out into the courtyard, by this time full of inquisitive faces and questioning neighbours. After some shouting among the gathering group, most of it aimed at the distraught husband, Elizabeth Harris, another courtyard resident, agreed to run up the street and rouse any men drinking in the Chequers public house. Some she would bring back, others she would send off to find both doctor and police. It was only a matter of minutes before the second of these two arrived at the house.

William Clark, parish constable and a man who had known the Addingtons all of their married life, having lived in Holcot for over twenty-five years, walked in through the door at a little after ten-thirty. By this time Mary had been lifted from the floor and placed in a chair, semi-conscious and by now fading fast. A quick assessment of her condition told him she would be not be able to help him solve the reason behind her certain death. So, ever a pragmatist, he turned his attention to Richard, who, still beside himself with grief and calling out to his now aphonic wife, had dragged himself into a chair at the opposite end of the same room. Meanwhile Francis Marshall, the local doctor, arrived and after confirming everyone else's prognosis decided it best to have Mary taken back into her own home. Organising a party from among the growing number of people clamouring to see the dying woman, he had her carried the short distance back along the courtyard. She died within half an hour of being moved.

According to the doctor's later testimony the neck wound had stopped bleeding by the time he arrived but her clothes were deluged in blood. After tearing away her dress he had found the two stab wounds Elizabeth Warren had been forced to feel by Addington. Both on the left side of her body, either wound would have proved fatal. One had penetrated deep into the chest, the other equally as deep but into the abdominal region where it had punctured the bowels. Marshall knew from examination and experience that they had been delivered with some force, which meant mitigating circumstances were going to be hard to substantiate.

*The Chequers pub, now a private house. (Author's Collection)*

Richard Addington, though, had no intention of trying to mitigate his actions. He appeared to be all too well aware of just what he had done and what the ramifications would be were he not to make some attempt at rationalisation. But despite being given the opportunity after being taken into police custody he remained stubbornly resistant. A thorough search of the Addingtons' house within an hour of Mary's death had revealed the murder weapon, a shoemaker's knife, heavily bloodstained and left where he had thrown it after the stabbing, on the kitchen table. No other signs of violence were evident. Police knew as they began questioning him that whatever had taken place in the house that morning had been quick and almost without any struggle. Beyond that they knew nothing, and other than Addington continually asking to see his now dead wife there was nothing else they were able to discover at that point.

At the inquest, held the following day in a room at the Chequers public house, county coroner, William Terry, heard evidence from all involved: in particular from those who had been drinking with him on the night before the murder. Because of the argument that had been overheard at around midnight it seemed logical to presume alcohol had been the cause and that its effects carried on into the morning. But no one who took the stand during that short hearing agreed with this hypothesis. It appeared that while Richard had stayed in the pub for some time he had only consumed two halves of beer, hardly a sufficient quantity to have warranted such an outburst. So in his summing up to the jury at the conclusion of the available evidence, Terry told the jurors to put aside motive and concentrate solely on who and how. These were simple enough questions to answer when the accused man had already essentially confessed in front of all his neighbours. Returning a verdict of wilful murder was therefore a foregone conclusion. After a brief, private hearing seven days later at Northampton prison this verdict was upheld and Richard Addington, by now having been formally charged with murder, was committed to trial.

The trial, before Mr Justice Byles on 14 July 1871, ought to have been an open-and-shut case. They had a victim, a body and a man who had never denied his guilt. Yet it proved to be otherwise. Ably defended by a Mr Merewether, the defence opened by telling the court that Addington had been insane at the time of the murder, that no blame could be attached to him for his wife's death because he had no idea why he had carried out the killing:

This was a most extraordinary case in which a man was charged with murder who was evidently possessed of affection for his wife. . . . It was contended on the part of the prosecution, that the prisoner committed the crime of murder with the knowledge that it was wrong to do it, and right to abstain from doing it. No doubt he committed the offence; he stabbed his wife in a most violent and aggravated way, inflicting wounds any one of which would have been sufficient to cause death. But there was no trace of a quarrel between the prisoner and his wife . . . if he knew what he was about, nothing more awful could be conceived against the laws of God and man.

It was probably the only defence available but proved both effective and difficult to dismiss.

Early evidence quickly established that twenty years earlier, when Richard had been in his late teens, he had suffered the misfortune of being kicked in the head by a horse. This was the foundation of the defence case, that up to that moment he had been perfectly sane, able to live a normal life, but that from that moment on his life had changed, the rules dictating his sanity blurred by his subsequent actions. Murder, they argued, was no more than a culmination, or climax, to a number of apparently unrelated events that when taken together showed it to be an inevitable outcome to his condition. It was sensible reasoning if it could be proved.

But Dr Francis Marshall, who had carried out the post-mortem examination of Mary Addington, had also attended her at the Warren house on the morning of her death and, it transpired, had also been the treating doctor after the incident with the horse in 1851, disagreed. He believed no such injury could have caused such a mental decline, that the wound failed to justify such a conclusion, that it could only be speculation. Unfortunately, as pointed out to him by the able Mr Merewether, he had no way of knowing that as fact. No medical science existed at that time that could have examined for any damage to the brain and he had carried out no follow-up assessment. The good doctor had to accede to this argument.

From that point on the defence counsel began to build its case, beginning with William Addington, Richard's brother. When he took the stand it was to tell the court that apart from isolated incidents that had taken place over the past twenty years it was the last three that had seen the greatest mental decline. The year 1868 he marked as being the start of what he believed was his brother's slow descent into madness. In November of that year Richard had decided that his wife Mary had begun an affair not just with his own brother but also with the policeman, William Clark, the man who made his eventual arrest. There was no foundation for the allegations, and after an altercation in the Swan Inn between the brothers Richard had been found, somewhat disorientated, in the backyard of William's house. He had no explanation as to why he had developed this sudden fixation and it was forgotten as quickly as it had arisen. But from that moment on, his brother insisted, he had continued to show a strangeness which often manifested itself in the company of others.

This ill-defined strangeness had apparently been witnessed by a number of men, particularly those who only met Richard through his association with a

*The White Swan Inn, 2003. (Author's Collection)*

village social club. Most of the men in Holcot were part of a social group that met on an irregular basis throughout each year but always came together for what was known locally as the Whitsuntide feast. This was held on Whit Monday at the Swan Inn and all the members paid 1s for the dinner, held at one o'clock in the afternoon, with all the beer paid for from contributions they had made over the past twelve months.

At dinners over the previous two years Richard had acted at times in a rather odd manner but on the feast held on Monday 29 May 1871, the day prior to the murder, his oddness had become more noticeable. A man not accustomed to public speaking, he had stood up at the conclusion of the meal as if to address the forty members in the room, waited for silence, then found himself to be mute and forced to retake his seat. An hour or so later he was found sitting in a window seat telling all who passed by that 'I have seen it'. What he meant by the phrase no one could ascertain because when asked to explain he again found himself mute. Seemingly unaware of how odd his behaviour had become he remained staring out of the window for some considerable time before leaving to visit the Chequers pub. Here he was found by a neighbour staring down into the bowels of the pub's cellar declaring that the landlord had taken his wife prisoner and was holding her in the darkness against her wishes. After some discussion he apparently agreed to leave and he and the neighbour walked quietly around the village. According to testimony at no time did he appear anything other than sober.

*Holcot church where Mary Addington was buried. (Author's Collection)*

Powerful stuff, asserted the defence – it clearly showed that Richard Addington was insane, that he had no control over his emotions, therefore no control over any subsequent actions. When he murdered Mary he had no idea why he had done so.

It may have held credence had it not been for the evidence of Mr Spurgin, the man whose responsibility it had been to supervise Addington's imprisonment during the six weeks or so since the killing. He told the court that he had seen nothing in the man's demeanour to suggest he was anything other than sane. At no time while in prison had he displayed any signs of mental derangement. Nothing, he maintained, had been displayed by Addington that supported the defence's argument that his prisoner had been, or was, insane.

In his summing up to the jury the judge told them:

The real defence was this – if defence there were – unsoundness of mind. It was necessary to explain more fully what was meant by unsoundness of mind before they went into the evidence. Partial unsoundness was no defence at all. There were many people walking about the world and engaged in the ordinary transactions of life whose minds were partially unsound. Now the soundness of mind which would exculpate a prisoner was of two sorts. The first was that if his mind was in such a state as that he did not know what he was doing, did not know that he was killing his wife or seriously wounding her: that would exculpate him. Or secondly, if he knew what he was doing, but did not know that what he was doing was wrong, that was a sort of unsoundness that would exculpate him.

The jury believed none of it. It took them only ten minutes to return a guilty verdict. Mr Justice Byles expressed no opinion of their decision as he placed the black cap upon his head and sentenced Richard Addington to death, though one or two in the courtroom did. There was a sense among those who had listened to the trial's progression that enough had been done to cast doubt on his state of mind. This in turn led to most inhabitants of Holcot petitioning the Home Secretary to grant a reprieve. Supported by their rector, the Revd Robert Montgomery, this petition was presented five days prior to execution but rejected. Undeterred, a further attempt was made on Sunday 30 July 1871 but again rejected and at eight o'clock the following morning Richard Addington made the short walk to the scaffold. His was the first execution in Northampton to be conducted within the prison precincts away from the public's often all too eager gaze.

# 5
# MURDER WITHOUT MOTIVE

*Towcester, 1873*

**W**ood Burcote Lodge farm lay about a mile outside Towcester, half a mile from the tiny hamlet of Wood Burcote and hidden from the main Towcester road by a series of old outbuildings. John Cox Newitt, a tenant farmer, had occupied it for just over twelve years, bringing up six sons and two daughters in the process. Known locally as a gentleman farmer, he had steadily built himself a reputation over the years for the quality of his produce, which had earned him a deal of respect among the business community, a reputation somewhat enhanced by his continual support of the church. Never churlish, even-handed with those in his employ and known as a man of charitable disposition, he had also ensured that his standing among those less fortunate was just as high. At seventy-one years of age, with four of his sons working the farm, he had undoubtedly reached a point in his life when work was beginning to take second place to retirement. Prospering through business and probably good investment meant that money was not in short supply. So, unlike many others living around him, he was able to take a step back from the day-to-day running of his farm and enjoy the leisure time life had afforded him. Without doubt, then, this ought to have been a successful and somewhat enviable retreat from the pressures of work. But John Cox Newitt had the misfortune to live too near to a man who cared little for repute.

Thomas Chamberlain had just passed his forty-third birthday when he moved into the toll gate house at Lords Field, a mile east of the farm and straddling the Buckingham road. It was a single-storey house with only two downstairs rooms: one a bedroom, the other a general-purpose room. Arguably he had been born into the job, since his birth at Long Buckby, some eight miles north of Northampton, had been inside a toll house and that was where he had spent his formative years. Brought up among the community of neighbouring East Haddon he had learned the rudimentary skills of managing a toll road from his father, who had taken over the toll house on the Northampton road. Whether at his father's insistence or not, at some point during the 1850s, while still living at home, he had also begun to work in the

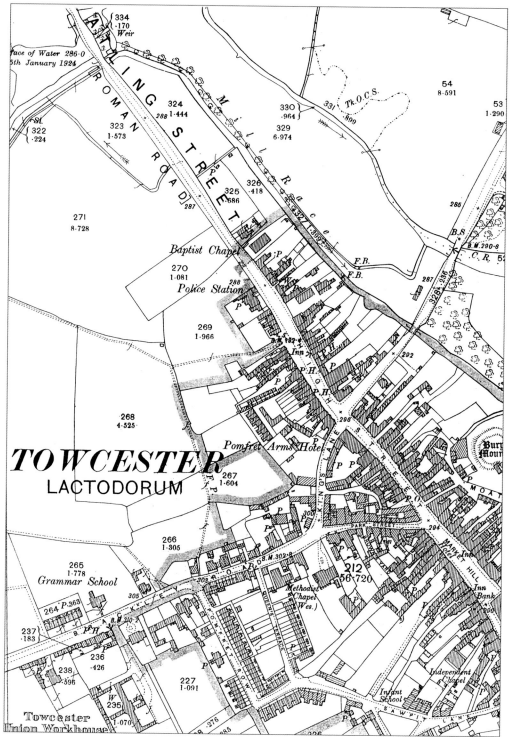

*Map of Towcester, c. 1900, showing the site of the Pomfret Arms. Wood Burcote lies north of the High Street. (Northampton Library)*

shoe trade and by the time of his marriage was a skilled shoemaker. It was a skill he maintained for the remainder of his life, though always working from home and using it to provide a subsidiary income; it is not difficult to understand why, as after a childhood spent in toll houses he would have known all too well just how poor an occupation toll-keeping was, though he didn't discount it as an occupation for himself. As an adult it was likely he would try to stay with something he understood well that was not too demanding on his time. It also solved the problem of housing. So, just as long as he was able to maintain his second income, the benefits of living on a toll road outweighed the disadvantages. The shoe trade therefore became a vital component of his working life.

But Thomas was in his thirties before he put this to the test, finally leaving home during the 1860s. Having been offered the chance to take over the gatehouse at Ravensthorpe he decided to take this easily transferable skill, along with his wife and two children, and set up home away from his father. In the main it appears they were successful, never financially secure but always earning enough to get by reasonably well and for them all to stay at Ravensthorpe until 1871. By this time the notion of toll gates was no longer as acceptable as it once had been and the job of toll keeper was in terminal decline, forcing men like Thomas Chamberlain to quit the occupation, give up their homes and find other work elsewhere or, alternatively, move around the

*Wood Burcote farm, 2003. (Author's Collection)*

county to wherever the work of toll keeper still existed. Thomas Chamberlain chose the latter. So it was that his time at Ravensthorpe came to an end and he arrived in Wood Burcote. Here, although the job itself only lasted twenty months before he had to move on to Lords Field, Thomas made the acquaintance of John Cox Newitt. For a short period during 1872, possibly because his shoemaking skills were not being sought out and money was a little tight, he had taken on some work for the farm. Over the period of a few months he had become familiar with its routines, its family and in particular its tenant farmer. There was never anything to suggest the relationship between them all was anything other than businesslike, or that the Newitts had found Chamberlain to be anything other than a conscientious and effective worker, but something certainly happened over those few months that made a serious and very marked difference to how Thomas Chamberlain viewed them, and on 30 November 1873 it manifested itself in the most horrific way possible.

It was a Sunday; for the Newitt family that meant attending church at Towcester in the morning, followed by a traditional lunch and an afternoon of relaxation. In the evening, as was their normal practice, the parents would stay at home while the rest of the family returned to church for the evening service. But on this particular Sunday a renowned preacher, a man Mrs Newitt knew well, had been booked to preach at that service and, unusually for her, she had resolved to go. Mr Newitt had no such compulsion and decided to stay at home as usual. So at around six o'clock he waved the rest of the family off and settled down in front of a good fire. The only other person in the house by this time was a young servant, Harriett Stevens, who remained in the kitchen ready to prepare supper on their return.

Between half past seven and eight o'clock that night she heard

*The toll house, 2003. (Author's Collection)*

someone enter through the farm front door, the only door to have been left unlocked. Presuming the family had returned earlier than expected, she stood up from the letter she was writing at the kitchen table and turned toward the door, expecting to greet them as they entered. What met her was totally unexpected. Thomas Chamberlain, a man she knew well, burst through the door, took hold of her and struck her a blow to the shoulder. She realised immediately that he was carrying a weapon of some description, but because the room was only lit by candle and firelight she could not see what that weapon was. He then struck her across the head; there was a struggle during which Harriett managed to push him away, forcing him back until he fell against a dresser. She screamed and John Newitt came rushing in. Chamberlain, recovering his feet, immediately attacked him and Harriett ran shrieking into the street. Half an hour or so later the nearest neighbour, Richard Darby, arrived with his three sons to find Newitt lying on his back in front of the fire, clearly dead, horrifically mutilated, and the kitchen of the farmhouse in a state of ruin. The old man and his fleeing servant had been attacked with a sword.

Superintendent James Osborne arrived at the Lodge at nine o'clock that night. According to his later testimony the blood spattered all around the kitchen showed that the fight Harriett Stevens had left behind had not only been violent, but had probably continued for some time after she had gone. In his estimation both men had fought across the full width of the room judging by the amount of blood shed and where that blood lay. There was evidence, too, to suggest the attacker had also been badly cut. Blood besmeared the back door and a trail led from the house to the road. The superintendent did the obvious thing and followed it for a total of 145 yards, at which point the trail veered off the road and disappeared for 40 yards or so before re-emerging from the fields and back on to the road. From that point on the trail was intermittent but sufficiently clear to take Osborne to the toll house on the Buckingham turnpike road. Thomas

*The road along which Thomas Chamberlain left the blood trail. (Author's Collection)*

Chamberlain was sitting by the fire when the superintendent entered the house. On a chair beside him was a jacket, heavily bloodstained, and in the bedroom a shirt, a pair of trousers and a waistcoat were all likewise soaked. Chamberlain, though, denied having left the house. Offering up his left hand, wrapped in a handkerchief, he told the policeman that he had cut himself badly while carving meat, hence all the blood and why he had changed his clothes. Ever fair, Superintendent Osborne found the meat, turned it over, satisfied himself that no one had cut anything from the beef joint that day and arrested him. As they left the house one of Chamberlain's children volunteered the information that their father had owned a cutlass, that he had brought it home two or three years earlier and that it was now missing. Osborne had a fair idea where it was. At the place where the blood trail had left the road was a pond, hidden from the road but known to most locals. He organised its search and within forty-eight hours the cutlass had been retrieved.

The evidence against Chamberlain was overwhelming, but he stoically refused to admit his guilt, insisting he had not left the toll house that night, that the blood found along the road had not been his and that the sword had been stolen months earlier. At the inquest held at the Pomfret Arms, Towcester, on the following afternoon Harriett Stevens was questioned at length over her identification of Chamberlain. It was pointed out to her that the Newitts' kitchen, which was a large room, had only been lit by a single

*The Pomfret Arms, c. 1900. (Wexford Transport Contractors)*

candle and the light of a fire. Was it possible she could identify the attacker as Chamberlain? Harriett was adamant she could.

Coroner: Did you know the person who came in ?

Harriett Stevens: Yes sir.

Coroner: Who was it ?

Harriett Stevens: (pointing to Chamberlain) I am sure it was him. I knew him by name before that time. He looked at me and I was going to call him by name and ask him what he wanted, when he caught hold of my shoulder. He had a weapon of some kind in his right hand and over his shoulder.

Coroner: When you went to Burcote did you tell [Richard] Darby who it was?

Harriett Stevens: Yes sir, I told him it was Mr Chamberlain from the toll gate.

This one piece of evidence was damning. In later testimony Harriett augmented it with an explanation of just why she was so certain she knew her attacker. Chamberlain had, it appeared, visited the farm on numerous

*Bradden church where John Cox Newitt was buried. (Author's Collection)*

*The Newitt family graves, Bradden churchyard. (Author's Collection)*

occasions over the past two years to deliver parcels left at the toll house. Each and every time he called it had been she who answered the door and she that had accepted them on behalf of the family. Harriett Stevens needed no more than candlelight to recognise a man she had known, albeit as a passing acquaintance, for so long a time. The coroner's jury agreed and returned a verdict of wilful murder against him.

At his trial before Mr Justice Brett in March 1874 Chamberlain stood in the dock and pleaded not guilty. Throughout his confinement he had never changed his story, insisting he had never murdered John Cox Newitt, that he had no reason to murder a man who had done him no harm, and that he had never left his house on the night of the attack. Mr Metcalfe QC, appointed by the crown to defend Chamberlain, mounted the only defence available to him, that of mistaken identity. Fraught with difficulty from the outset he attempted to prove only two facts. One, that the blood found on the clothes taken away from the Chamberlain house could not be proved to have been Newitt's and two, that Harriett Stevens was mistaken. In the first he scored an easy success. No scientific test existed in 1874 that could differentiate between two blood types. So, the blood discovered could just as well have been his own and could have been caused by a knife slipping while cutting meat. But in the case of the identification evidence he was on less certain ground. Despite his strong cross-examination of the young servant he could not force a retraction, nor was he able to distort or create any kind of ambiguity in her evidence. Dispassionately Harriett told the court, as she had the inquest, that her recognition of Chamberlain was sure and certain and, as the coroner's jury had done three months earlier, the jury returned a guilty verdict.

Chamberlain remained obdurate throughout the remainder of his imprisonment, which lasted only for two more weeks. Executed on Monday 30 March at Northampton he remained silent as to his motive, appearing to those who met him during his final days to be unconcerned as to his fate. He made no attempt to fight the court's sentence and never discussed the murder from the day he walked from the dock to the day he mounted the scaffold. Officially, motive for the murder was logged as robbery, but unofficially police believed the motive to have been notoriety. Thomas Chamberlain wanted to be famous, if only for a short time. John Cox Newitt had simply been unlucky.

# 6
# THE PRICE OF MADNESS

### *Stoke Bruerne, 1885*

Thomas Brookes had lived all his forty-four years in or around Stoke Bruerne. Never marrying, his had been a life dominated by his parents, which in turn had bred a degree of resentment. From time to time this resentment had bubbled to the surface, resulting in arguments with his father, Charles, a man whose stature belied his seventy-four years and who was used to having his own way. These arguments were often fierce and more often than not brought about by Thomas's frustration at having to live at home. All too well aware of her son's dissatisfaction with life and his volatile nature, it had therefore become his mother's role to act as arbitrator between the two men, a role she had grown both accustomed to and accomplished in as the years had gone by. It was also a role Thomas had grown to appreciate. But when she died and her place, as he saw it, had been usurped by the housekeeper, Mary Webb, his sense of resentment knew no bounds. This all came to a head after being forced to leave his job as a guard on the railways during 1884.

At some point that year his father had fallen critically ill; so ill, diagnosed his doctor, that recovery was almost impossible and death more or less a certainty. Aware of this likely outcome, his father asked that Thomas stop working on the railway and stay at home to nurse him. This was a life-changing decision for Thomas and one that he was initially reluctant to make. Only after a discussion with Richard Orpen, the doctor who had made that diagnosis, did he agree. But it was an agreement made with the knowledge that the cottage in which he lived, rented from a local landlord, would be assigned to himself when he left his job, not after his father's death. Quite rightly, he wanted to know that he could continue living where he had spent much of his life. It also gave him a status he had never enjoyed before. But medicine in the nineteenth century was an imprecise science and Charles Brookes made a complete recovery. This left Thomas in a rather invidious position. With his father back to full health and resuming his position at head of his household this new-found status had been somewhat diminished.

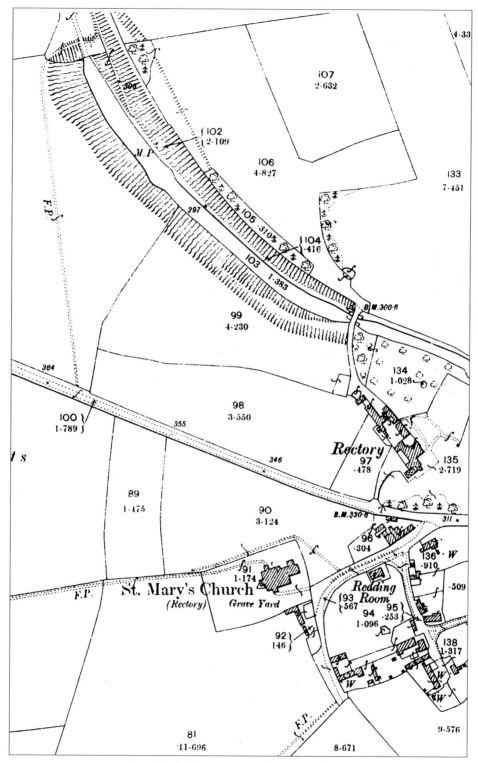

*Map of Stoke Bruerne. (Northampton Library)*

The two men were almost instantly at odds with each other. Charles tried to assert his right to take back the cottage in his name, as it had been prior to his illness. But Thomas refused; he was not about to relinquish his elevated standing within the community and saw himself as a man with rights, which gave him governance over the house and those who lived within it. He was not about to give that up. Neither was his father.

In January 1885, after weeks of quarrelling with each other, Thomas finally snapped and physically attacked his father. Being younger, Thomas inevitably won, and Charles suffered two broken ribs as a result. But it resolved nothing. Neither father nor son was about to move out of the cottage; there was little choice and even less money. Both knew they must remain together, but for Thomas the damage had been done and he considered the antagonism between the two could never be resolved. The relationship, as he saw it, was in terminal decline and he wanted no part in it. He decided, perhaps as a protest, that while he would sleep in the house he would not eat in it. So began the final act in a tragic drama.

Over the past few years Thomas had carefully nurtured a relationship with neighbours, the Tites. Ham Tite, a widower, had a 24-year-old daughter, Mary Ann, who kept house for him. Young, attractive and single as she was, Thomas was almost certainly smitten, seizing any opportunity he could to call at the house just to talk. Mary Ann, on the other hand, was a discerning woman who was no doubt flattered by his attentions but who possibly saw him as an older, mature and less interesting man than those she met during the normal course of events. Whether Thomas was ever aware of the impression he had created is not known, but as no serious relationship ever developed it is probably fair to surmise that he was. Either way, he continued the visits and after this serious falling out at home it was to the Tites that he turned.

*Footpath leading into Stoke Park Woods, 2003. (Author's Collection)*

*View of Stoke Bruerne Old Rectory, c. 1901. (Author's Collection)*

Ham Tite had no objection to him deciding to eat with them on a daily basis provided they did not have to cook for him. Thomas agreed, quite happy to allow his father's housekeeper to continue with this role. So each day he collected his meals between two plates and carried them the short distance to the Tites' dinner table. The arrangement worked well. Thomas was able to stay out of the family home for much of the day, there was less animosity between him and his father, and he got to spend time with Mary Ann. To any who knew him he appeared content at having solved a problem that for a time had seemed irremediable. But secretly, deep inside, he was far from content. On Tuesday 3 March 1885 this growing sense of disquiet finally erupted.

Arriving at the Tites' during the morning he had resolved to spend the day with Mary Ann. She had no objections; he had done so before and had never caused her any concern. The day passed without incident and at seven o'clock that night she left to attend a meeting at the local school. Thomas sat for an hour by the fire talking to Ham Tite, then said he would wander off down the road to listen to this meeting through an outside window. After an absence of half an hour or so he returned. It was now after eight-thirty and Ham wanted to go to bed. Working as a labourer took its toll and he began to complain at his daughter having agreed to attend a meeting that would keep him up until late. Thomas sympathised, offering to stay up and wait for her if he wished, but Ham would have none of it. Not because he mistrusted Thomas's intentions – there had never been anything to suggest that Thomas was anything other than honourable when it came to his daughter – but Ham was her father and fathers waited up for their children. So for the next hour the two men sat in comparative silence, watching the fire, until she returned at nine-thirty. The minute the front door opened Ham was on his feet and after a few brief words he left the two of them downstairs and went to his bed.

Thomas now became difficult and argumentative. Irritated at her staying out so late he snapped at her. She in turn, piqued by this sudden and unprovoked belligerence, snapped back. But by this time Thomas was not a man to be argued with. Putting a hand in his pocket he pulled out a revolver, stolen from among his father's belongings, aimed it at her head and fired once. He then walked calmly out of the house, careful to retrieve the two plates that had held his dinner that night, crossed the street and entered his own cottage. The housekeeper, Mary Webb, met him at the door; having heard the shot she thought it had begun to thunder. As he pushed past she asked him if it had started raining. Putting the two plates into her hand he told her no. Somewhat disbelieving she looked out into the street, then followed him in. As they reached the centre of the room Thomas turned back to face her, lifted the gun toward her and pulled the trigger. Seeing his intentions in time, she instinctively raised a hand – dropping the plates – and deflected the bullet which grazed the top of her head. Charles Brookes, suddenly aware of what was happening, jumped from his chair beside the fire and helped grapple his son to the ground. The gun went off again, wounding him in the hand, before Thomas was able to wrest himself free. Then with the gun pointed at his own head he shot himself. Believing the shot to be fatal and satisfied that his housekeeper had only sustained a superficial wound, Charles stumbled out into the street, and ran across to the Tites' house.

Mary Ann sat in the armchair beside the fire. Blood poured from a wound just behind her right ear, saturating her dress and completely covering the upper part of her body, but she was still alive. Dazed, but without any assistance, she stood up as Charles Brookes ran into the room and walked calmly across to the sofa. He and Ham Tite tried to stem the flow as she told them how Thomas had shot her. Charles relayed the events from his own cottage and told her Thomas was dead on the floor of his sitting room.

He was wrong. Despite having fired from almost point-blank range, Thomas had failed to do himself any real damage, partly because he had loaded the gun with lead shot and partly because his aim had not been true enough. Within minutes of Charles and his housekeeper having run outside he was on his feet and fleeing the scene. But while this lead shot had been his saviour, for Mary Ann it was to prove the opposite. The shot had penetrated her brain to a depth of some 6 inches, scattering shot and bone as it went. The fact that it had not killed her outright was simply down to luck. Unfortunately for her, though, this luck would not endure. No medical skill existed at that time capable of removing shot from so deep inside the head, nor could doctors stop the bleeding. Mary Ann was destined to linger on for some days without any hope of recovery.

Meanwhile Thomas Brookes had made for nearby woodland. The head wound he had sustained was not serious enough to cause him any lasting damage. Knowing the area around Stoke Bruerne well he made for Stoke Park Wood, an area of woodland that would offer him the best chance of evading capture in the short term. Police were on the scene within an hour of his disappearance and with the help of local people launched a search of the immediate area. By dawn they had found nothing and a search was being considered in a different, wider area. It was at this juncture that Brookes, having spent an uncomfortable night in the open, fired two shots, both aimed at himself and either designed to kill him. Once again he bungled the attempt – the first missed and the second rendered him unconscious. Police were on him within minutes. Bundling him on to a makeshift stretcher they carried him back to his father's house where he was placed on a mattress and his wounds attended to.

In the place he had chosen to spend the night, hidden among brushwood at the centre of the wood, police found letters and bills, most torn into pieces, and above, where he had slept, a piece of card was pinned to an oak tree. While many of the letters were of a personal nature, some had been scribbled over and others patently written that night. These were of particular interest because it was plain that Thomas Brookes had had no intention of ever returning to Stoke Bruerne. It was equally obvious that suicide had been his intention from the minute he ran away from home the previous night. Believing he would be found dead, these documents were a summation of his actions and the motives behind them, and therefore vital evidence.

*Stoke Bruerne village, c. 1901. (Author's Collection)*

On the piece of card Thomas had written: 'All this lays at Chas. Brookes's and Mrs Webb's door.' And on an envelope torn in half, which he had not cast aside but placed into his trouser pocket, he had written out his confession:

> I have never spent a happier night in all my life. I was so pleased to hear old Polly sing [Mrs Webb?], as I came out of the door. I do hope and trust that Old Bruit Mrs Webb is done for. I have made my piece with my God all these have been such bruits to me and the old man can never prosper.
>
> 3 a.m.
>
> TB
>
> Old Charley cannot hang me now.

Other letters attacked his father, critical of his involvement with the Church and declaring him to be the Devil. But the most sinister was a note written days earlier regarding his sister, Elizabeth Eyles. Married, she had moved to the village of Ravenstone after her wedding, a move Thomas had welcomed. According to the note he believed her to be 'a nasty mischief-making thing and eaten up with poor pride'; more importantly he had decided upon a date for her death, 26 February 1885, which he had crossed out and amended to 3 March 1885 – the day he had shot Mary Ann Tite. It was enough to convince police, at that juncture, that perhaps she had not been the intended victim. A theory was hurriedly put together based upon what had been found, that Brookes had taken the gun that night from among his father's possessions, intending to murder three people, housekeeper, father and sister, at which point he was to kill himself. It seemed a rational, sensible explanation of the night's events, yet the police also knew that if he had amended that date after the shootings then perhaps he had believed Mary Ann to be his sister. Conjecture, perhaps, but as no mention of this young woman had been found among any of the writings Brookes had made while waiting for dawn, they knew it could have been possible.

As this speculative theory was being advanced Brookes was being taken to Northampton Infirmary. Mary Ann Tite on the other hand had been left where she lay, at her father's house, to await her inevitable death. Superintendent Norman, of Towcester police, having taken over the investigation, decided in view of her injuries to take a deposition while he could and to that end arranged a magistrate to join him at Ham Tite's home. Mary Ann was fully conscious when they met and after relaying the events of the night as best she could told them that the motive, as far as she knew, was jealousy. Brookes, having gone down to the school on the night of the meeting, had seen her through the school window talking to a young man he knew. For that, she believed, he had shot her. Two days later she was dead.

*Stoke Bruerne church where Mary Ann Tite was buried. (Author's Collection)*

Thomas Brookes was not so fortunate; he made a full recovery. On 26 April he stood in the dock before Towcester magistrates charged with murder, his head swathed in bandages, but otherwise with an appearance of general good health. The wounds he had sustained, according to the hospital doctor who had treated him, were mainly superficial. He had used shot, which, unlike in his victim, had not penetrated far into the scalp, and all were easily removed. After listening to witness evidence from the families involved and from the post-mortem examination carried out by Dr Orpen, there was little choice but to return a guilty verdict and send Thomas to Northampton's assize court for trial later in the year.

The trial opened three months later and Brookes pleaded guilty. It was a futile gesture. The moment Brookes sat down his defence counsel, Mr Harris, told the court that he had failed to impress upon his charge the severe implications of the plea he had just made. In his opinion, he insisted, Thomas Brookes was therefore not fit to plead. After some legal debate it was decided to allow a jury to decide if this were the case. Doctors who had examined him closely while in prison were called to give evidence and unanimously agreed that throughout these examinations Brookes had exhibited clear signs of being delusional. He was, in their opinion, unaware of the reasons behind his trial, was suffering from melancholia, and had lost much of his mental capacity owing to a fracture of the parietal bones of the skull. Their evidence was enough to convince the jury and the trial was brought to a halt. Thomas Brookes was sent to a mental institution for life.

# 7

# THE BODY IN THE
# BAG MURDER

## *Northampton, 1892*

Wh                  hen Charles Hadley went poking about in a ditch with a stick he could
never have imagined his actions would be the cause of Northampton's
greatest mystery. Indeed, had 7 August 1892 not been so hot he would never
have clambered into the ditch in the first place. Only the heat, which he
believed had caused the ditch to smell so abominably, compelled him to begin
a search of the bordering hedgerow alongside the Althorp to East Haddon
road (now the A428).

Convinced that the body of a lamb lay at the bottom of the 5-foot drainage
ditch, probably having fallen in and died trying to escape, he set about
locating it and pulling the corpse out. Egged on by others who had endured
the growing stench for some days but who were not brave enough to go in
search of its source, Charles, having no such qualms, was all too eager to
waste a few hours on a quiet Sunday though it was far from easy, the
hawthorn being fairly dense and with a nettle bed running across the ditch's
uppermost edge. But nothing was to deter the determined explorer, and
having once clambered into the adjacent field he set about his task with some
enthusiasm. After some few minutes his stick had parted the tangled
undergrowth and he could clearly see what he thought to be the shorn back
of a dead sheep. At that point his courage deserted him. Nauseous, he decided
it better to leave the animal *in situ* and fetch out East Haddon's local police
constable, who was best placed to cope with such an ordeal – it went with
his job.

The next day, when Police Constable Dench climbed into the ditch, the
weather had broken and heavy rain swept across the fields behind him. Seeing
through the undergrowth had become that much more difficult, which meant
little was gained by way of probing. All he wanted to do was get the job over
with and return to the warmth of his station. So, without ceremony, the
moment he saw the white back of what he believed to be a dead sheep, he
grabbed hold and pulled. Unfortunately for him what eventually surfaced
from beneath his feet was far from the expected animal.

# A NORTHAMPTONSHIRE MYSTERY.

## A Woman's Body Found on the Roadside.

## BUTCHERED AND BEHEADED.

### Ghastly Details.

## A HORRIBLE CRIME.

A fearful discovery was made on Sunday on the roadside not far from Althorp railway station, the headless and armless body of a woman, tied up in a sack, being found secreted in a ditch. The body was in a frightfully decomposed state; indeed, it was on account of the fearful stench arising from the ditch that led to the shocking discovery. For several days at the end of last week passers by, even those in traps, noticed the abominable smell that arose from the ditch on the left-hand side of the high road from Northampton to Rugby, a few hundred yards beyond Althorp Station. There is a good footpath on the right side of the road, and none on the left side, where the body was deposited, and few foot passengers, therefore, passed very close to the place. Those who suffered from the stench concluded

Northampton Mercury *headline from 12 August 1892, which first alerted the town to the mysterious discovery of a headless corpse. (*Northampton Mercury*)*

The white, apparent newly shorn, fleshy back turned out to be a white sack tied at its neck, heavy and seeping with moisture. Dench hauled it on to the bank beside him and carefully began to pick apart the string holding it together. Once it was unfastened he took hold of the bottom corners, turned it upside down and emptied out the contents. Tipped out in front of him was a second bag, this time made from coarse canvas and again tied at the neck. Now aware that what he had at his feet was something far more dubious than a dead sheep, he became more tentative in his approach. Turning the bundle, which was about the size of a coal sack, he carefully felt along its bulk looking for any clue that would betray its contents. There was none and, having been joined by this time by seven or eight curious men, all of whom wanted the bag opened, he was persuaded to ignore police protocol, cut away the knot and just upend it. What they then discovered both appalled and sickened, probably in equal measure.

Inside was the armless, headless torso of a woman. She had been wrapped in a green skirt, nightdress and a long piece of linen. The legs had been drawn back behind the torso until the ankles touched the buttocks and had been tied in place. Partly dressed, she wore a chemise, drawers and black stockings but had on no shoes. Every part of the body had also been smeared in lime, presumably to speed the rate of decomposition. The upper part of the body, the chest and shoulders, which had not been covered, had certainly suffered considerable degradation as a result, much of it having been destroyed by a combination of insect infestation, lime and general putrefaction brought about by the hot weather. A hurried search of the area revealed nothing else and the constable sent two men off to find a doctor and others to locate his superintendent in Northampton. Meanwhile, he mounted guard over the remains.

Dr Churchouse, surgeon, of Long Buckby a mile or so away, had been visiting his father-in-law in East Haddon and was quickly found. He was at the scene within half an hour of the partial body's discovery. Not that there was a great deal he could add to what everyone had already seen. Once satisfied the head and arms were not in the same ditch, he had the body stretchered to an outhouse at the Red Lion, East Haddon. Here, closer examination revealed the woman to have been around 5 feet 5 inches tall. The dissection, he believed, had been carried out by someone in possession of rudimentary medical skills who also knew a little of human anatomy. A heavy knife or small hatchet and probably a saw had been used.

This was not a great deal for Superintendent Alexander – who had arrived at East Haddon just after the body's removal – to go on in the early phase of his inquiry. The height fitted almost all the women in Northamptonshire; no head meant no easy identification and lack of forensic scientific knowledge in the 1890s prevented any accurate calculation as to time of death. But what he did have was a label: no ordinary label either. After the body had been removed from the field Constable Dench had carried out a thorough examination of the sacking in which it had been found. That had revealed a luggage label. The label was common to the railways, had a stamp for L&NWR along its bottom edge and written clearly across its centre 'E.M. Rae, Northampton'.

Diligent police work over the next few days revealed that the label had been attached to the sacking by a London company, Warren & Sons, bacon and cheese merchants. They in turn dealt with the Northampton wholesale

*Althorp railway station, c. 1950. Annie Pritchard's body was found some 800 yards away. (Stations UK)*

company, based in Crick some five miles north of East Haddon, owned by Edward MacRae, a farmer and provision merchant with a high street retail outlet at Daventry and a warehouse at Dychurch Lane, Northampton. The sack had been used to carry smoked bacon by rail and MacRae's was the only outlet in Northamptonshire with whom the London company traded.

Edward MacRae confirmed all this, willingly assisting the police investigation, telling them that bacon had been arriving every week at his Northampton warehouse bagged in such a way until 20 June 1892. After that date sacking had given way to boxes, which had made transporting quantity much easier. The bacon, still in its sacking, was sold through the Daventry shop as would have been expected up until the changeover, but MacRae also owned a market stall which sold meat products on Northampton market, run by his brother Andrew. He told police that bacon had continued to be sold there in sacks until early July. Andrew MacRae confirmed that to be the case, adding that hundreds of sacks bearing such a label had been sold by his stall in the previous six months alone. The obvious conclusion was that any one of those hundreds of buyers could have used the sack to carry the dead woman to East Haddon, a fact not lost upon Superintendent Alexander who knew only too well that unless he found something else his investigation would grind to a halt almost before it had begun.

That something else came to light after a routine police inquiry at the railway station at East Haddon had revealed a postcard, handwritten,

*The Red Lion where Annie Pritchard's dismembered body was taken after its discovery. (Author's Collection)*

instructing the railway to collect a number of items from a house in Birmingham. In itself not significant – instructions of that type were made every day – but it was believed this particular one had been written out by Andrew MacRae in March that year, and though by this time the police knew he had a home in Birmingham the address set out for collection was different. When Birmingham police called at the house, simply as a matter of routine to confirm the collection had been made, they found the home of the Pritchard family: what's more, a family who had not seen a daughter since the time of that collection. Suddenly Andrew MacRae became interesting.

The more the police delved the more they uncovered. It transpired that MacRae had a wife and child at home in Birmingham and for some time they had all lived next door to the Pritchards; 31-year-old Annie Pritchard, the missing girl, had known him well, too well – according to one of her brothers. There had been some trouble toward the end of the 1880s over what the family considered to have been improper behaviour by their neighbour. As a result the MacRaes had moved. The collection made by the railway, the Pritchards confirmed, had been Annie's clothes and personal belongings packed into two tin boxes plus a portable sewing machine.

As far as they were aware she had run away with a man called Guy Anderson, a man she had met some years earlier and someone they had all known previously. The family believed that it was he who had organised the collection because Annie had told them she was off to New York, as the two were to be married. Confirmation of all this had arrived home in a letter, dated 28 March 1892 and postmarked Liverpool. Fortunately they had kept this letter. When police began questioning in earnest they produced it as corroboration for what they had believed for months. The letter was genuine enough; they all vouched for the handwriting, certain it was Annie's, and pointed to the fact that she had sent for her clothes: all perfectly logical for a woman going to America. What was not so logical, however, leastways to the police, was the fact that it had been Andrew MacRae and not Guy Anderson who had sent for those clothes. Even more mysterious, the clothes had never arrived in Liverpool but at 33 St John's Street, Northampton.

Here, police discovered that the two tin boxes and the sewing machine had arrived on 19 March 1892. On the following day a man known only as Mr Anderson and a woman matching Annie Pritchard's description had moved in. They stayed for seven or eight weeks living as man and wife, moving in mid-May to a house two doors away in the same street, owned by Sarah and Henry Pilkington, again living as man and wife and using the name Anderson.

Further investigation of the MacRae family revealed that Edward was the business head of the two brothers. Residing and working in Northampton, he had built up his business alone and only involved Andrew in March after he

St John's Street, Northampton, where Annie Pritchard and Andrew MacRae had lived together. The photograph was taken in 1960 just prior to its demolition. (Author's Collection)

had become aware that he was out of a job and looking for work. Installing him in the Dychurch Lane warehouse as manager, he had also given him responsibility for the market stall in Northampton's market square. Andrew's wife and family, who had no wish to move, had remained in Birmingham to where he would travel infrequently for the odd weekend. It was an arrangement that everyone involved appeared to have accepted without a problem. When they questioned him about his association with Annie Pritchard, Andrew MacRae denied any impropriety had ever taken place but made no attempt to hide the fact he had known her, though not, he insisted, for a number of years. As for transporting her clothing by train he insisted that police must either be wrong or his name had been used in error.

But the evidence against MacRae was beginning to build up. Throughout August, after comprehensive coverage of the crime by virtually every newspaper across the county, people were coming forward with more and more evidence of his involvement. As a market trader his face was known to many of those who either traded or bought at Northampton's open market. In turn this meant his movements could be pieced together like a jigsaw puzzle. Slowly police were able to uncover sufficient evidence to show that he had known Annie Pritchard, that she had been in Northampton since March 1892, that for some five months he had been living a dual life and that she had been part of that dual life. What they had not been able to prove was that the body in the ditch was hers or that she had been murdered. They never would.

What they would be able to prove, though, was that Andrew MacRae had lied, not just about his association with Annie but about his knowledge of her whereabouts throughout her time in the town. If, ran the argument, he had lied about this then in all probability he had murdered her. The breakthrough came in early September. After four weeks of intensive police work the investigating team had uncovered a number of key pieces of evidence. The first was that he had been responsible for moving her clothes from Birmingham to Northampton: his handwriting was found to be identical to that found on the railway's postcard request. The second was positive identification by photographs from both owners of the rented houses in Northampton where police knew Andrew and Annie had stayed, confirming that Andrew had indeed been the man who had lived with her since March. Finally, the clothing found on the body was confirmed as belonging to Annie after being identified by her family.

So as August came to an end the police knew the body, even without identifying evidence, was almost certainly that of Annie Pritchard. The clothing her family had confirmed as being hers could not possibly lead to any other conclusion being drawn. But even if MacRae had lived with her could they prove that he had killed her, dissected her body and thrown it into a ditch? This was the stumbling block. MacRae had constantly denied any knowledge of the woman, despite the mounting evidence to the contrary, arguing that as a trader in the town he would be known by any that used its market – a fact not lost on the police. However, a third breakthrough came from two different sources at the beginning of September.

Because of all the publicity MacRae had become, in a short period of time, a sort of macabre celebrity. It was this growing notoriety that brought a woman named Sarah Pulley into Northampton police station with a story that, for the first time, helped pull all the various strands of the Pritchard and MacRae relationship together. Annie had been pregnant. According to Sarah, she had delivered the baby, a boy, on 23 June at the house on St John's Street. As a result of this unexpected testimony Andrew MacRae, police began to speculate, must have moved her from Birmingham for one reason and one reason only – he had little choice. He could not afford his wife to know that he had been having an affair with their former next-door neighbour. She in turn could not risk her own family discovering her pregnancy, and so a plot was hatched. They would bring back Guy Anderson and fake an elopement. It seemed a perfectly rational explanation but was there any irrefutable evidence to prove it?

There was, and it came from Mrs Louise Bland. On 23 July Andrew MacRae sold a number of dresses to her at her second-hand ladies' clothing shop in Northampton. He claimed they had come from his wife who had been committed to a mental institution and were no longer needed. She had retained the clothes, and after reading of an appeal for information had decided to come forward. Subsequent identification by Annie's sisters was enough to prove the link. Andrew MacRae was arrested and charged with murder on 3 September.

While in police custody it was also discovered that twenty-four hours prior to selling the dresses MacRae had changed address; he had moved from the house he and Annie had shared to a house at 68 Derby Road where Sarah and William Philpot took him in as a single tenant. He had also sold a tin hat box, three books and a bible inscribed 'Linda Pritchard' to Robert Morrell, an antiquarian dealing in any personal items that he could sell on. Once it had been confirmed that Linda was the name of Annie's younger sister the noose tightened around his neck.

On 21 December MacRae stood in the dock of Northampton's courthouse before Mr Justice Kennedy and pleaded not guilty to murder. The defence case from the outset was simply that regardless of his involvement with Annie Pritchard no evidence existed which could, beyond doubt, prove that the partial body recovered from the ditch near East Haddon village was hers. Nor, they insisted, could it be proved that the body found had been murdered or had ever given birth to a child. Their contention was straightforward enough    if the prosecution believed Andrew MacRae to be responsible for murder then they must prove it.

*No. 68 Derby Road where Andrew MacRae went to live after the murder. (Author's Collection)*

This was exceptionally difficult to do. The post-mortem examination carried out by Dr Churchouse was inconclusive. All he was able to say with any degree of certainty was that the body was definitely female. The upper part of the body was so denuded of flesh that the bones had all fallen together when lifted. Heart, liver, lungs and stomach had all perished over time, which meant ascertaining cause of death was impossible. So was time of death. In view of the decomposed state of the body, exactly how long it had been in the ditch could not be stated with accuracy. All he was able to tell the court was that the head and one of the arms had been severed using a saw. Defending barrister Mr Attenborough had set the scene at the outset of the trial and never allowed the jury to forget that proof of murder and victim identity just did not exist.

What did exist, though, were enough witnesses to show that Andrew MacRae had been around Annie Pritchard through most of 1892, including a man whom Annie had met at Northampton railway station. James Felley told the court that while waiting for a train to Liverpool she had approached him and asked if he would post a letter for her from Liverpool station. He agreed, took the letter, which had a Birmingham address, and did as she asked. The date he knew to be 28 March. This letter, with its Liverpool postmark, was intended to deceive, to ensure the Pritchard family believed the assertion that Annie had gone to America. Prosecuting counsel, who used this to open their case, then brought to court all those who had been associated with both Annie Pritchard and Andrew MacRae between March and July 1892, thus building a chronological calendar of events through their evidence that could not fail to impress the jury as to the certainty of the prosecution case. The final witness in this list, Harriett Burrell, told the court that on 20 July 1892 Annie Anderson, as she knew her, had visited her house to bring her a portable sewing machine. Harriett needed it to carry out some repairs to dresses she owned. According to her, Annie had stayed at the house for several hours, along with her baby boy, and had been collected by Mr Anderson, whom Harriett believed was her husband. This man she clearly identified as Andrew MacRae. When the two left the house they had walked off in the direction of Dychurch Lane. This, claimed police, was the last day of Annie Pritchard's life; no sightings existed after that date and Dychurch Lane was where both mother and child had been murdered.

Unfortunately they could not prove it. Weeks had been spent examining the warehouse in Dychurch Lane. All knives and saws had been confiscated. The cellar floor had been pulled up and the drains emptied. But they had found no conclusive proof to back the claim that this was indeed the murder scene. Their difficulty was simple: the building had been used to store bacon joints, all of which were always washed, some cut up and others boiled. Anything found – and some small bones were discovered in a drain – could not be confirmed to have been human.

Northampton Mercury's *headline of 9 September 1892 after* Andrew MacRae's arrest. (Northampton Mercury)

*Northampton Courthouse, c. 1890. (Northampton Library)*

At the end of five long days, during which forty-five witnesses had taken the stand, the defence claim made at the outset, that murder and identity could not be proved, held good. The judge in his five-hour summing up reminded the jury that the body found in the ditch had not been established as that of Annie Pritchard, nor had time or cause of death been ascertained. What had been proved, however, was Andrew MacRae's association with her and in particular over the final months of her life. It took the jury one and a half hours to decide that this association was enough and they returned a guilty verdict.

Pandemonium broke out in the courtroom, with Edward MacRae having to be physically removed as he protested his brother's innocence long and loud, while outside the huge crowds that had gathered in anticipation of just such a verdict broke out into spontaneous cheering as the news was relayed to them from the steps of the courtroom. Mr Justice Kennedy, after waiting patiently for several minutes until order was restored, turned toward the dock and asked if MacRae had anything he wished to say. He did, and after repeating his innocence he turned toward the jury box to pronounce his own verdict.

*East Haddon church where Annie Pritchard was buried and is reputed to haunt the churchyard. (Author's Collection)*

Gentlemen you have this day, each and every one of you, become what you have made me – a murderer. You have this day widowed a good devoted wife; you have this day, this night, this Christmas eve, made fatherless loving children. Go home to your homes, can you with a clear conscience? Have you in giving your verdict tempered your duty with mercy? I say no. As long as you live, your conscience will accuse you.

It was a short but powerful speech, though it made no difference to the sentence passed. Over the next few days there was feverish activity in organising a petition calling for his sentence to be reduced, citing Mr Justice Kennedy's closing speech to the jury as being sufficient to show that the evidence produced was purely circumstantial; evidence of a type that should never condemn a man to death. It had little impact. When news confirming the sentence of execution was given to Andrew MacRae he wrote a last letter home. It was a letter in which he admitted having seen Annie, a fact his wife by this time must have been well aware of, but in which he tried to explain what had happened to her and why.

Dearest Wife,

Knowing as I do how truly innocent I am of the crime for which I have been condemned, I cannot but feel how awful it would be if such a miscarriage of justice should take place and my having to suffer the extreme penalty of the law for an offence which I have never committed. The greatest reason I should not do so is because I am sure sooner or later the mystery will be cleared up by the supposed murdered person returning, or her friends hearing from her.

For my own part, for a right I know she must be alive and well. I have no doubt of this as far as I am concerned. The jury went into the box prejudiced toward me, with their minds made up as to the verdict. They took not the slightest notice of the learned judge, who was decidedly in my favour, and would, if left to him, have acquitted me.

The evidence as to the clothes worn, presumably by Annie Pritchard, on the night when last seen, is entirely false . . . she never went or ever saw the warehouse. She left that same evening for London to meet Anderson from Castle station, Northampton, at 8.35. She took with her all she thought necessary. I did not see her again but on the evening of the day following I received a few lines from her telling me not to send the things she left, but to sell them to help to pay several little bills she had left. Thus I did so openly, and without fear.

She was in communication with this man, and on the afternoon of the 19th July told me she had received a letter from him from London, part of which she read. It stated that he should come for her on Thursday. Thus her determination to go at once. Both you and I knew of Guy Anderson. He was in Birmingham in November last year. The Pritchards knew all about him. This they kept back. What I did was out of kindness for an old and esteemed friend. If I die I shall die innocent.

Fondest love
Andrew MacRae

Innocent or guilty? Either way, Andrew George MacRae was executed at 8 a.m. on Tuesday 10 January 1893.

# 8

# THE PRICE OF INNOCENCE

## *Sulgrave, 1897*

Francis Smith had endured a difficult few years after his wife had died, especially being left alone to raise four children. Splitting his day as best he could he managed to hold down his labouring job by starting early in the morning, returning home at midday to cook a meal and then being back at the house again by dusk. Grateful for help from any quarter, which he called upon infrequently and only then as a last resort, he worked hard at trying to keep his family together. Having lived in the tiny village of Sulgrave, south of Northampton, for much of his life offered up certain advantages. He knew most of his neighbours, the majority of whom it would be fair to say he trusted. So leaving his children to others when time or work made unexpected demands was not necessarily a difficult option. Nevertheless he made every attempt to keep these occasions to a minimum, helped in this by his son Albert, aged thirteen by the summer of 1897, who had begun to take on a more adult role in the household at a younger age than most of his school friends. It was a task he had accepted willingly enough, especially when helped by his only sister, Alice. At nine years old she had probably begun to see her brother in a new light and wanted to share in his new-found responsibilities. They were inseparable, and a familiar twosome around the village. This close bond between brother and sister also meant that wherever they went they were invariably seen, a situation they may have found irksome but one that proved fortunate after the events of 10 July 1897.

There was no means of locking the cottage door while their father was at work. A simple nail or splinter of wood pushed through the narrow aperture between door and frame easily lifted the latch. That afternoon the family had a visitor who did exactly that to gain entrance to the house.

James Shaw was uncle to the children but not a regular visitor. He had spent the last seven years as a private in the Scots Guards, only receiving his discharge papers eight days earlier. Visits to see his nephews and niece over the past ten years could therefore be counted on the fingers of one hand. So when he turned up unexpectedly, letting himself into the house at around two

*The road out of Sulgrave that Albert Smith and his uncle, James Shaw, walked along on 10 July 1897. (Author's Collection)*

o'clock in the afternoon, they were quite possibly excited at seeing him again. It was a fine day, and when he suggested they set out on a walk through the fields bordering the narrow road to Helmdon some two miles away, it seemed a sensible suggestion and they readily agreed. Like Francis, his brother-in-law, James had been brought up in and around Sulgrave and knew the topography of the place reasonably well, particularly the footpaths that criss-crossed much of the land, which at that time of year was high in barley and oats. Like most children he knew they would jump at the chance to be outdoors and if being outdoors meant going on some huge adventure so much the better.

After leaving the house Shaw took them to Mr Godfrey's shop in the village and bought them sweets, a treat for going out with him. He then walked them down the Helmdon road toward what was known locally as Stone Pits field. Here they all climbed over the wooden fence bordering the road and ran off into the oat field. The group was seen by local beat bobby Fred Cole who knew the family. He had watched them as they came out of Sulgrave and for a while walked ahead of them as they made their way toward Helmdon village. According to his later testimony they were all in high spirits and enjoying the day, but at some point that afternoon things changed.

When Francis Smith arrived home at a little after six o'clock that night he found only Alice. She told him that Uncle James had sent her home some hours earlier but that her brother Albert had been allowed to stay out. Not reading anything suspicious into that – it was still light outside – he made himself and Alice something to eat. It was not until around eight o'clock that he began to search for his son. A quick tour of the neighbourhood revealed nothing, so he ventured out along the same road that Alice told him they had taken that afternoon. The search area widened as the night went on, with friends and neighbours joining him, until, at around 2 a.m., it was decided by all concerned that it had become too dark to continue and the search was abandoned for the night.

On the following day, Sunday, after another abortive attempt to find Albert, Francis sent his elder brother across to Banbury where he believed James Shaw to be living. Sarah Hobbs, James's sister, had lived there since her marriage and in the light of James's recent discharge from the army Francis knew this was the only place he could have gone. He was right. The message came back that Shaw had left Albert outside Sulgrave's blacksmith's shop at around four o'clock the previous day. In itself it was a meaningless piece of information – Albert could have walked anywhere from there, in any direction. Francis called in the police. They organised a second search, which lasted for most of Sunday and found nothing. So Constable Fred Cole, the constable who had seen the group together on the Saturday, brought Alice out on to the Helmdon road and asked her to show him just where she had been when Shaw had sent her home. She took him to a spot beside an oat field roughly midway between Sulgrave and Helmdon. Pointing into the field she told him that just beyond the wooden fence was where she had left her uncle with Albert. Some 50 yards or so in from the road Cole found a place where the oats – which were then grown to a height of almost 6 feet – had been trampled down; a place where someone had sat or lain down. Leading out from this flattened area toward a ditch, which he knew bordered the field, was a narrow path of broken grass stems. Satisfied he had found the spot Alice had described, Cole then followed

*The view toward Helmdon from the area of the murder site. (Author's Collection)*

this trail of broken stems until they opened out into another, wider area of flattened grass that eventually gave way to a steep bank. At the bottom of this, in a ditch, lay the headless corpse of Albert Smith.

When Dr Thomas Hickling climbed down into that ditch some two hours later rigor mortis had already set in, and in his estimation the boy had been dead for more than a day. Lack of medical expertise prevented a more accurate estimate being made, but as he viewed the body at around half past ten at night at least police knew the murder had taken place at some point on Saturday. Not far from where the body lay a cut-throat razor was also found, wrapped in a piece of blood-soaked paper, which when opened out had upon one side a line drawing of Cleopatra's needle. The drawing was later identified by Alice as being hers and something she had given to her brother. The head, covered over by grass, lay in the same ditch but some 7 feet away. It was also clearly evident from the flattened area around the top of the bank that there had been a violent struggle. Blood, which covered much of the hedgerow above the murder site, had also pooled in two distinct areas, which led police to believe that the struggle had ranged across a 10- or 12-foot area. Albert Smith had fought hard for his life.

At around the time that the body was being examined, Alice Smith was telling Constable Cole that while she had been in that field her uncle had assaulted her. Whether or not her brother had seen it happen she was unsure; the oats were so high as to hide anyone who lay down among them. She thought that Albert had gone on ahead of them and that when Shaw lay her down he was not nearby. This, she told the constable, was why she had been sent home. James Shaw was arrested within the hour and charged with murder, though at the time of making the arrest there was no hard evidence to link him to the crime other than that of association: he had spent time with the children during that afternoon, had been seen in their company and the surviving child had accused him of a sexual attack. It was enough.

Early the following day, Monday, an inquest was opened at Sulgrave's schoolroom to determine the facts behind the case and to ascertain whether or not a jury would accuse James Shaw of the killing. The evidence against him, circumstantial as it was, left little doubt to those who heard it. Having had time to carry out a more thorough examination of the victim, Dr Hickling told the packed room that the cut-throat razor, though blunt, had severed the head, that great force had been used in order to accomplish the act and that the boy had been beaten, possibly during a running fight. Francis Smith confirmed that the razor was his, that it had been in its place on the mantelpiece when he went to work on the Saturday and was missing when he returned home on Saturday night. Alice reiterated her story of assault and a total of three independent witnesses testified to having seen Shaw and the children together that afternoon. It took only ten minutes to return a verdict of wilful murder.

*Helmdon railway station, c. 1940, where James Shaw went after the killing. (Stations UK)*

But James Shaw insisted he was innocent. He told police that when he had said he had left Albert at the blacksmith's shop that had been the truth. There was no possible way, he insisted, that he could have committed the murder because he was in Banbury, had travelled back there by train from Helmdon that same afternoon. Unfortunately for Shaw too many people had seen him during the course of that warm Saturday afternoon – enough to build a timetable of events around the crucial hours. Signalman Alfred Hobbs remembered him as the man who came looking for a train at 3.45 p.m. He recalled a conversation the two had over Saturday's timetable, described Shaw very accurately, and recollected that after being told there would be no train until after five he had asked about a train from Brackley. The village of Brackley was about a seven-mile walk and Shaw managed to do it in just over an hour and a half, boarding the 5.22 from Brackley station to Banbury. A passenger on that train, and a man who shared the same carriage, was Police Constable Samuel James who had no difficulty in identifying Shaw after his arrest. But it was not these two men that provided the most telling evidence against him, but two more policemen.

The first had spotted him at half past one on Sunday morning in Sulgrave, and the second some three hours later, this time in Banbury. Why, the investigating police officers wanted to know, did Shaw travel all the way back from Banbury in the early hours of the morning and then make the long walk back again before dawn? He had no explanation, but they did. The theory that had evolved as more evidence emerged was that he had murdered Albert at around three-thirty on Saturday afternoon. Panic caused him to flee the scene before he could hide the body properly. Aware that a search for the body would have been mounted, he therefore returned to the scene in the dark to make an attempt at hiding Albert before he could be found. Unfortunately for Shaw searchers were all around him, shouting out to each other as they went, which prevented him from succeeding. So, they argued, after throwing the head and torso into the ditch all he was able to do in the dark was cover the head with grass and then run away again. He walked home simply because there was no train at that time in the morning and as an ex-soldier he was physically very fit. As a theory it held together very well and when Shaw came to trial they put the idea before the court.

Mr Justice Wills, who sat in judgement on 19 November 1897, heard the evidence with a sympathetic ear. There was really no doubting Shaw's guilt but what was in question, and he knew it from the outset, was his mental state. Mr Hammond Chambers, who stood for the defence, produced a line of witnesses designed to show it was far from being sound. James Shaw's mental condition, he told the court, had been in almost terminal decline since his birth. According to medical evidence his father had attempted suicide three times by using a cut-throat razor and once by attempting to drown himself. None had worked but, ran the argument, Shaw had inherited a mental condition that was totally unavoidable, and he was insane. To back up the theory Chambers brought a number of men into the court who had served with the defendant for much of his army career. They were all able to show that over the years Shaw had developed a delusory tendency, often manifesting itself in him holding conversations with imaginary people. As the condition had worsened so too had his tendency to become violent. While in prison awaiting trial this violent side of his nature had become apparent and was witnessed by a number of prison officers. But no matter how sound the argument, or how conclusive the medical

*All that remains of the entrance to Helmdon railway station, 2003. (Author's Collection)*

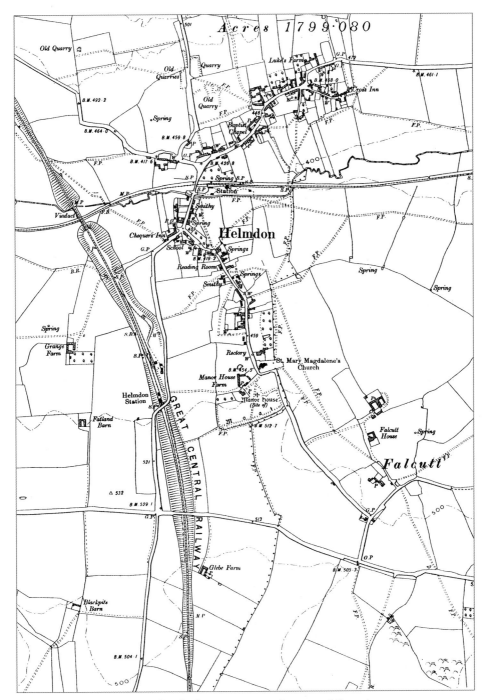

*Map of Helmdon, 1900. (Northampton Library)*

evidence, the jury of twelve men refused to bend to the notion that James Shaw was anything other than sane. They returned a guilty verdict. Placing the black cap upon his head Mr Justice Wills had no choice but to sentence him to death.

Within hours of Shaw leaving the dock a petition was being launched to try and have the sentence commuted to one of life imprisonment. Two eminent London doctors were brought in to examine Shaw and determine his sanity. On 1 December, eleven days later, that reprieve was finally granted and Shaw was declared criminally insane.

# 9

# A DEADLY RELATIONSHIP

Mary Elizabeth Meadows was a woman in love. She had met the man of her dreams during 1895 and for four years the two had been almost inseparable. By March 1899 marriage had already been discussed and her family expected the two to set a date later that year. Money, or lack of it, was probably the only area of their relationship that held them back. Mary had been in domestic service for most of her adult life but had never been able to secure any sort of working stability. Domestic servants were not hard to come by for most households and companies. It paid little by way of a wage, could never be considered to have any permanency as a job, was extremely hard work and had no serious future. But for Mary the positions were relatively easy to find, provided she placed no restriction on their locations. Familiarity with Northampton meant this was rarely a problem; having lived in the town all her life there were few places out of reach of easy travel. Moving from job to job had therefore become almost a way of life. Lack of a good wage, though, had no doubt caused her some concern, particularly in the light of a hoped-for marriage.

However, Josiah Cornelius Parker, the man in her life, had never expressed any concerns over her fluctuating fortunes. Neither had he seemed too keen to offer marriage to Mary. Four years was certainly seen by some as having been a long time together without the possibility of a wedding. Yet it was no secret the two had been sleeping together whenever opportunity allowed, and most of Josiah's free time was spent with Mary at her mother's house on Salisbury Street, Semilong, where she still lived. So it was quite likely he viewed the idea of marriage with a cynical eye, deciding he had all the comforts of home without any of the responsibilities. Either way, outwardly he showed no signs of being unhappy with either their relationship or the situation they were in. But Josiah Cornelius Parker was far from being the man everyone believed him to be.

Since his birth his parents had hidden a secret they hoped would never see the light of day: a secret they considered so devastating if it were known that

*Salisbury Street, Kettering, 2003. (Author's Collection)*

they had maintained a silence throughout all their son's growing years, carefully monitoring his progress through adolescence, watching for the tell-tale signs that would have confirmed their worst fears. But there had been none. At the age of twenty-four it seemed he had escaped the affliction that had devastated most of his family across the generations. Unfortunately they must also have known that unlike any normal illness the condition they had guarded against often betrayed no outward signs until it was far too late. Insanity was an illness unlike any other and they had had first-hand experience of it. Six members of his mother's family had been committed to mental asylums. On his father's side it had been almost as bad, his grandfather having committed suicide as a result, and three others having also been committed. So they had good reason to be concerned. Mary, apparently oblivious to these facts, had none.

On Friday 10 March 1899 an apparently happy, content Josiah Parker walked into a gun shop on Bridge Street, Northampton and bought himself a revolver for 5s. He gave no explanation for the purchase and told Mary Dickens, who ran the shop with her husband, that he was experienced with firearms. Producing a pistol from his pocket he then explained to her why he wished to replace one with the other, and according to her later testimony she had no reason to disbelieve him. What happened to this second gun is unknown, but certainly by the end of the day he had disposed of it, possibly through a pawn shop of which there were many in Northampton. Either way

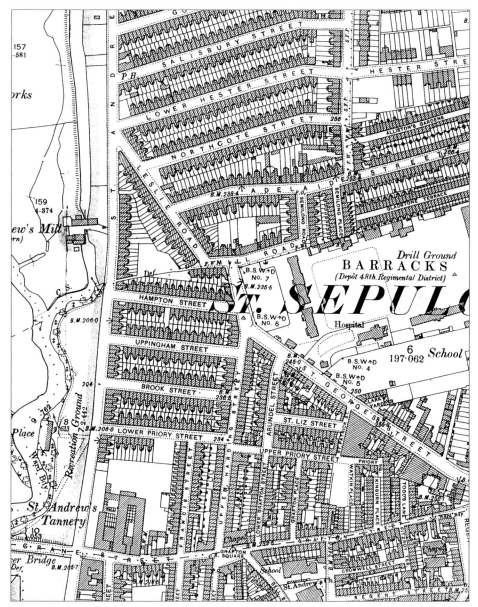

*Map of Northampton, c. 1900, showing the terraced street areas around Salisbury Street. (Northampton Library)*

she understood it was not a gun he intended to keep, buying only cartridges for his new revolver before he left the shop. The revolver he kept on his person, probably inside his jacket pocket, for the remainder of the day. After work he met Mary and the two went out drinking, returning to the house on Salisbury Street at around eleven that night, he somewhat inebriated, she comparatively sober. After drinking what remained of a jug of beer Mary's mother had left on the kitchen table he was persuaded to stay the night, as Mary was concerned that his being drunk would upset his landlord if he returned home. So she made up a bed for him on the sofa and told her mother she would stay downstairs with him. The two were left together for the night.

At a little after five in the morning Mary's mother heard tea being made and presumed that Mary was making an early breakfast. The household was normally up and about between five and six in the mornings so there was nothing unusual in hearing them moving around. Half an hour later she heard them leave the house by the back door. George Jelley, on his way to work in Kingsthorpe, passed the two of them walking toward St Andrews Road. He remembered Mary because she had stopped him to ask the time. It was twenty-five minutes to six. Looking back he saw they were arm in arm heading off in the direction of Spencer Bridge Road. A minute later, no longer, he heard two shots.

A young woman on her way to work at a local brick factory found Mary lying on the pavement just beyond Semilong Working Men's Club. Blood poured from two bullet wounds, close together, just above the right ear. Just as she began screaming for help Josiah Parker walked up to Police Constable Ward Marlowe, two streets away in Royal Terrace, and asked him if he would like a job to do. Offering up the revolver he told the policeman he had shot Mary twice in the head, where he had left her, and the fact that she was dead. By the time police arrived at the scene, which was only some five minutes after the shots had been fired, that certainly was the case. As the later

*Bridge Street, Northampton, 1900, where Josiah Parker bought the gun he used to murder Mary Elizabeth Meadows. (Northampton Library)*

*Semilong Working Men's Club. Mary's body was yards from the main door. (Author's Collection)*

post-mortem showed she had stood absolutely no chance of surviving what were two very well-aimed shots, the bullets having travelled the whole substance of the brain, coming to rest against the inside of the skull opposite to their point of entry. Death had been near enough instantaneous.

Parker told police it had been a suicide pact. The two of them, he claimed, had decided over the course of the previous night they would kill each other. He insisted that Mary had asked him to shoot her. The only reason he had not done so while the two of them were at the house on Salisbury Street was because they would have been heard by Mary's mother. It had been his suggestion that they left the house early and walk to a place where he thought it best to carry out what were meant to have been two killings. Just why he had not followed through after Mary's death and killed himself he could not explain.

At the inquest, held at the Duke of York public house, Salisbury Street, later that same day it transpired that after shooting Mary the first time Parker had caught her before she fell, then gently placed her on the pavement so as not to bruise her. Believing her to be still alive he had then placed the muzzle of the gun just above the first wound and fired a second shot. This he felt had killed her. Intent on maintaining her dignity he had then placed her hat, which had fallen off, back on to her head and calmly walked away. Police speculated that he had shot her while walking beside her, still arm in arm. It was doubtful, they believed, that she would ever have known what was happening to her. Parker had ensured this by the manner in which he had carried out the killing. He had also accepted his guilt from the moment he had handed the gun to the officer he had met within minutes of carrying out the murder. But from the witness evidence produced he had never intimated to anyone that he had harboured any such intent. Hours later he was in court, formally charged with murder and remanded until the summer assizes.

Three days later, Tuesday 14 March, thousands began gathering along the streets of Semilong from late morning, all wanting to participate in some way in the funeral of a woman whose death had clearly moved them. People were densely packed in places along the route intended for the little funeral cortège, some having been to the house to view Mary's body in her coffin, others satisfied just to witness the event. They remained silent as three horse-drawn coaches carried the polished elm coffin swathed in flowers toward St Paul's Church, followed by the family. Here police had been brought in to help control the growing numbers and keep the gates to the church clear. But the crowd was well behaved and readily moved to allow the hearse access. All remained outside while the service was carried out, then formed a long, snaking procession behind the coffin as it was carried on its final journey to Kingsthorpe cemetery. According to the *Northampton Mercury* some 3,000

*St Andrews Road in 1961 just prior to its demolition. (Northampton Library)*

*The Duke of York pub. (Author's Collection)*

people massed around the cemetery gates, their heads bowed in respect as the cortège passed them by. Then, once the family had left the graveside, they filed silently past the still open grave casting flowers, mainly lilies of the valley, on to the coffin.

No surprise then that crowds also thronged the streets of Northampton at the opening of Josiah Parker's trial, though probably not with the same sense of sadness and certainly without any sense of forgiveness. Most in Northampton had no sympathy for Mary Elizabeth Meadows's murderer. This perhaps was one crime where they almost collectively demanded justice, a sentiment possibly understood by Mr Justice Lawrence when he took his seat late in the morning on 23 June but certainly not one he would have allowed to influence his court.

Parker, on the other hand, had great sympathy with the public's cause and had no intention of allowing the court to produce any evidence that could mitigate his actions. He pleaded guilty. There followed a legal debate. Parker, obviously aware of what he was doing and the inevitable consequences that were likely to follow, had to be persuaded to change his plea. He was reluctant, and only intervention by the judge forced his hand. The judge also appointed a defence barrister, Mr Magee, on Parker's behalf.

From the outset the defence argument centred around insanity. Once the line of witnesses had been paraded before the court to show that Parker had shot Mary – which was undeniable – a motive had to be found. Nothing any witness told the court gave rise to any belief that the two of them had argued or fought with each other at any time previously. On the contrary, all the evidence produced led the court to believe that they were almost the perfect couple. No one witness had been able to testify that anything in their behaviour could have led to Parker taking such appalling and tragic action. Therefore, argued Mr Magee, it must have been an act of insanity. Aware of the family history, it was his strong contention that Josiah Parker had begun to suffer the family's curse. To that end he brought a doctor, William Harding, medical superintendent of the Northampton County Asylum, to the court. He was the man who had decided Parker's fitness to plead and who had closely observed and reported on Parker throughout his incarceration while awaiting trial. Mr Magee wanted to know if, in his opinion, Parker had been insane at the time of the murder:

Dr Harding: An insane man may exhibit no symptoms of insanity at one time, and be in paroxysms of insanity at another. Insanity is hereditary to a very great degree. If a man exhibited symptoms probably due to insanity in the family, the probability was the greater that the symptoms were due to insanity.

Mr Magee (referring to the report acknowledging family history): And your own expression in your report was that it was 'a terrible history of insanity?'

Dr Harding: I know of no other equal to it.

Mr Justice Lawrence: What do you say was his condition at the time he committed the act?

Dr Harding: I consider he was suffering from one of his suicidal impulses, a form of suicidal insanity.

The insanity card had been played and had the witness evidence ended there possibly it would have carried the day. But Mr Lee Cogan, prison doctor, had also had Parker under his watchful eye and he did not agree. According to his evidence Parker had exhibited no signs of insanity while in prison. Furthermore, he did not share the view that insanity had been the cause of the killing. But Mr Cogan was not a mental expert, as Mr Magee adroitly pointed out to the jury, a fact he insisted they did not overlook. Whether or not they accepted the point is debatable. After retiring for only ten minutes they returned a guilty verdict but did add a strong recommendation to mercy on account of insanity within the family. But it was not enough to prevent the judge from donning the black cap and pronouncing the death sentence. Parker – immaculately turned out, wearing a well-starched red and white shirt front with gold studs, a high starched collar, a dark green bow tie and a black jacket – stood up in the dock to receive his sentence in an almost matter-of-fact manner. He then thanked the judge and was led away to the cells.

The attitude of the town changed almost within hours. Once details of the case and Parker's family history had been published, those who had clamoured for the full penalty of the law to be applied were beginning to have a change of heart. Letters began arriving at the *Northampton Mercury* calling for the sentence to be commuted to life imprisonment. The Home Secretary, in light of the jury recommendation and Dr Harding's testimony and report, had two doctors sent to Northampton to carry out a full mental examination of Parker in order to assess whether commutation was a valid option. Unfortunately for Parker they found no signs of insanity and the petition for reprieve therefore failed.

Josiah Parker, meantime, showed no signs of concern. Indifferent to his position he apparently maintained a healthy appetite throughout, slept well and appeared content with the verdict. In a letter to his landlord, Harry Hopkins, he tried to explain this apparent sense of the inevitable.

> When I was being tried, my heart was beating like a clock pendulum and I was thinking of you when I was in the dock. I was not surprised at the death sentence. I was prepared for it. God has helped me through the trial, and now I hope he will help me through the last. . . . I feel sure I have got to die, and I trust God will help me through . . . I shall never forget you while I am living, which I don't think will be long. I hope I shall die happy, and that God will help me to bear up, for my time is short.

Perhaps this fatalistic approach was borne out by his knowledge that he had always intended to murder Mary Elizabeth Meadows. In a reported conversation he had while in prison he seemingly stated that he had intended to kill her on the Friday but because they had both gone out drinking he had put it off until the Saturday morning. Suicide had never been his intention. Whether or not this was true, on Tuesday 11 July at eight in the morning he paid the ultimate price. A crowd of over 5,000 gathered outside the prison gates. From their vantage point they could not see the execution but as the clock struck the hour, in the ensuing silence they could plainly hear the bolt drawn that released the trap door beneath Parker's feet.

# 10

# WITH MALICE AFORETHOUGHT

Alick Claydon could be said to have been unlucky in his parentage. Born in Northampton in 1858 to a drunk and a mad woman, by the age of ten his father had committed suicide by cutting his own throat and his mother had developed the first signs of schizophrenia that would eventually send her to a mental asylum. Education had played almost no part in these early years, which meant that by the time Alick reached young adulthood he was able only to write his own name. Reading came a little later, largely self-taught, but he was never able to progress much beyond the headlines of a newspaper.

In his early twenties, despite this poor start in life, he had met and fallen passionately in love with Louisa, a young woman for whom literacy came second to the ability to earn a wage, and Alick was certainly able to do that. From a very young age he had been apprenticed in the shoe trade and by the time he met Louisa was earning well as a shoe finisher. The two of them became inseparable, and were thought by most to be so perfectly matched that marriage was a certainty. But they were wrong; for whatever reason the two fell out, drifted apart and the relationship crumbled.

Louisa eventually married another shoe finisher and became Mrs Wareing. Moving to Portland Street, Northampton, they had several children, though all except daughter Kate died young. Despite these tragedies the marriage was, in the main, successful. Working in certain areas of the shoe trade at the end of the nineteenth century produced a generous income, and because Louisa had developed the same skills and worked equally as hard as her husband their financial situation was certainly healthier than most. This success meant the two had money to spend and, as Robert Wareing liked a drink, their social life began to revolve around the local pubs in the area. He was undoubtedly a heavy drinker, and although Louisa was essentially teetotal, the sobering influence, they both spent long hours staring into a glass, and their children began to suffer for it. Often left to fend for themselves, they would call on neighbours for food and drink. They in turn, tired of the parents' neglect of their children, would call out the police to find

*Portland Street, Northampton. (Northampton Library)*

the parents and bring them home. Inevitably tensions were high at times. Only Louisa's sobriety and acts of arbitration prevented these all too frequent events from escalating to the point where they would have been forced out of their home.

Into this situation during the late 1880s walked Alick Claydon. Having not seen Louisa since their break-up he too had married. At the time the Claydons moved into 7 Portland Street, some twenty-odd doors away from the Wareings; they had no children but were hardened drinkers – just the kind of people Robert Wareing was drawn to. The four inevitably became firm friends, spending time in one another's company, either in their own homes or in the various pubs around the area. This went on for several years until, after a particularly heavy night's drinking, Robert, in a drunken stupor, fell over in the street, hit his head on a kerbstone and died. The consequences of his death upon Louisa were catastrophic. As the main wage earner, Robert's money had paid the rent; without it she and Kate, her only surviving child, now around ten years old, were likely to be evicted. Alick and his wife came to her rescue and offered to let her lodge with them; as the Claydons had a second bedroom it was hers if she wanted it. Louisa had no hesitation and moved in within days of her husband's death. The four of them remained, almost as a family, for the next year or so after which Alick's wife unfortunately fell ill and died. This left Alick and Louisa in a difficult situation: to continue living in the same house would have been viewed with distaste. Inherent within Victorian society was a moral code not recognised today that would have seen their relationship as unseemly at best, corrupt at worst. It seemed a sensible solution that the two former lovers should agree to marry.

Unfortunately for Louisa, the man she married was no longer the man she had known all those years earlier. Sharing a house as a lodger was one thing but as a wife it was quite something else. Alick Claydon had become a man made up of two very distinct characters. On the one hand he was a very expert shoe finisher, a quick workman who was capable of earning very good money. When in the mood to work he was a brisk, active, intelligent man, someone careful of his appearance, somewhat vain, always well dressed, his shirts always white and laundered, his jackets tailored and tight-fitted. But when not in the mood to work he invariably drank to excess, became indolent, listless, somewhat sullen, with a tendency to remain unshaved for days. A binge drinker, he became a man who would simply drink until all his money had been spent, then return home, wait until sobered up and begin work again. These mood swings Louisa found impossible to handle and the strains on their marriage worsened by the year.

Toward the end of the 1890s the shoe industry in Northampton made changes that heaped further misery on this already strained relationship. It was decided that all shoe finishers must work from inside a factory and not from home. Furthermore, the jobs of women finishers were abolished. For the Claydons it was a decision that brought severe financial hardship. Alick, who had spent all his life working from a back room in his house, would not work from a factory. The earnings burden he simply passed to Louisa. She in turn threw him out of the house and took in washing, the only way she could provide an income for herself and her daughter. The two lived apart for just over a year, during which Louisa had Alick in court on three separate occasions claiming maintenance, none of which he paid, until finally she agreed to allow him back home because it was the easier option. By this time of course the marriage was essentially over, Alick was drinking more and more and she had grown further away from him.

By the summer of 1901 she had resorted to locking him out of the house for long periods during his all too frequent drinking bouts, forcing him to sleep under hedgerows or on park benches. Unable to stop himself, he had grown ever more resentful of her and whenever the two met they clashed. These confrontations, while non-violent, escalated to such a degree that they were almost a daily occurrence. Unfortunately for Louisa what she never realised was that Alick was capable of far worse.

On 7 July that same year, after yet another week of sleeping rough, Alick sat in the bar of the Old Globe, having run out of money yet again, searching for a face that would buy him another beer. Out of the corner of his eye he saw Louisa walk in carrying a basket full of clean laundry. Situated at the top of Portland Street, and with Louisa living only a few doors away, the pub had employed her to wash all its dirty linen. On his feet before she could rest the basket on the bar, he hesitatingly asked if he could come home. Probably out of sympathy for the condition he was in, Louisa agreed.

At around eleven that night he walked back into the house for the first time in many days. Reluctantly Louisa fed him, gave him something to drink and then went to bed. Reeking of beer, unshaved and having not washed for days, Alick simply followed her. Inevitably the two had a row in the bedroom. Incensed he should want to share her bed after so long and in such a state she protested vociferously, calling him names and trying to bar him from the room. Alick was having none of it. After so long sleeping in fields he wanted his bed back and he was going to have it. Though reluctant, there was nothing Louisa could do to prevent it and so, having lost the argument, she turned her back on him and went to sleep.

Just after one in the morning Alick Claydon awoke from his drunken slumber. Apparently wide awake he pushed himself out of bed, walked out on to the short landing and into the back room used as a workshop, picked up a heavy rasp file – a common tool in the shoe trade – and returned to the bedroom. Louisa, still sound asleep, had not even stirred. Without a moment's hesitation he walked around to her side of the bed and proceeded to beat her to death with the file. Eight times in all he smashed the heavy tool against her head, two of the blows shattering her skull, then gripping it across its widest

*Moulton village, c. 1900. (Northampton Library)*

*The Telegraph, Moulton, in 2003. (Author's Collection)*

part he used the spiked end, which had no handle, to stab her repeatedly. Death was almost instantaneous. After satisfying himself that he had killed her he then lit a lamp, walked downstairs, fried himself two eggs, which he ate with bread and butter, returned to the bedroom and slept beside the battered corpse until 4 a.m. He awoke with the first streaks of daylight, and with no sense of remorse he put a hand against his wife's body to judge if she was cold. Satisfied that she was he then climbed out of bed and calmly left the house.

For the next two hours he walked, finally ending up in the Telegraph Inn at Moulton where he met Joseph Lack at a little after nine in the morning. The two men, who knew each other reasonably well, sat outside in the pub yard and drank a beer. Claydon, perhaps troubled by his conscience after all, suddenly found himself unable to keep silent about the night's events and began to tell Lack, in detail, what he had done, finally showing the palms of his hands, still blood-soaked, as verifiable proof of the murder he claimed to have committed. Lack had no reason to doubt Alick's story, particularly after seeing his hands. The two men then discussed at length what ought to be done next. Claydon talked of suicide and produced a knife from his pocket, explaining that it had been his intention to cut his own throat. But Lack saw nothing in the man's demeanour to suggest the threat was credible and told him to put the knife away and just surrender himself to the police. Almost as if relieved, Claydon agreed, provided he could have a last beer. Lack put his hand in his pocket one last time and the two sat in silence until their glasses were drained. At a quarter to ten that same morning Alick Claydon met Constable Bailey on the street in Moulton village and confessed to the murder of his wife.

Initially disbelieving, the constable asked him if he could prove such a serious accusation. He said he could. Unbuttoning his waistcoat he held it open to reveal the shirt beneath saturated in Louisa's blood and then held out his still bloodstained palms. It was enough. Taking Alick to the nearby small police station he sat him down, explained the seriousness of what he had said and the likely consequences if true. Alick appeared to show no concern and proceeded to make a full statement:

> Last night I met my wife at the Old Globe public house on the Kettering road. I remained there until 11 p.m., and then went direct home and up to bed. . . . My wife was in bed. She called me a dirty dog and would sooner have a serpent beside her than me. I did nothing, I said nothing. I then went to sleep and slept until about 1 a.m. I believe I got up and went into the shop and got my file, and struck my wife with it on the head . . . I could not say how many times I struck her. I then went and ate two eggs and some bread and butter. . . . I then went back to bed and went to sleep till a quarter to four, when I awoke.

After making this statement he was taken to Northampton's county police station. A search of his person revealed a shoemaker's knife and two pawn tickets, neither significant. The murder weapon they would find later where

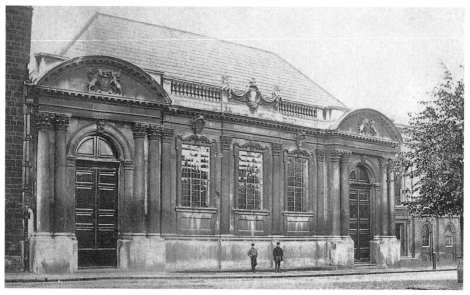

*Northampton Courthouse (Shire Hall) where the trial took place. (Northampton Library)*

he had left it, lying on the bed beside the dead Louisa. Kate, his stepdaughter, unaware of the night's events, had already found it by the time this search had been concluded. Pushing open the bedroom door at a little after half past nine that morning had revealed the full horror of her mother's murder, the body lit by the early morning sun as it streamed in through the room's only window.

This discovery, which Claydon knew he had left for Kate to make, appeared not to have given him one moment's concern. For this reason, perhaps more than any other, it also ensured that his statement would damn him. Its content revealed murder and its detail had been given in an apparently sober, dispassionate way. So detached from its consequences had he become, particularly those involving Kate, that many around him that morning viewed him with real abhorrence. There could be no mitigation for so callous an act. The possibilities for courtroom defence of his actions were also severely weakened.

Just over three months later, on 21 November 1901 at ten in the morning, those possibilities were put to the test. Standing before Mr Justice Bigham in Northampton's Shire Hall, Alick Claydon pleaded not guilty to the charge of murder. With no legal representation, the judge had instructed Ryland Adkins to act on his behalf and mount whatever defence he was able. He chose that of insanity, believing that the murder had all the hallmarks of being carried out by a man stripped of his sanity at the time he had carried out the killing. No one, he argued, could possibly have had control of their mental faculties and then carried out an attack in the way he had upon his wife. Ignoring the early witness evidence involving post-mortem, timing, discovery and weapon, all of which he appeared to have concluded required no legal challenge, he focused upon Alick Claydon's family, in particular his parentage. He wanted to reveal the background to the man's childhood to the court and use it as a means to imply insanity.

Besides detail already known concerning Claydon's father, Ryland Adkins had also uncovered little-known facts regarding other members of the Claydon family, in particular two cousins who had been placed in mental asylums at various points over the previous ten years and an uncle who had committed suicide in Africa. Added to this was the further unknown fact that Alick himself had attempted suicide when only seventeen years of age. This, Adkins told the jury, provided clear evidence of a sure and certain legacy inherited by Alick from birth. He had always had a tendency toward insanity.

Unfortunately for the defence case, Dr William Harding, medical superintendent of Northampton's Berry Wood Asylum and the man who had agreed with such a contention in the Josiah Parker trial two years earlier, this time found himself in opposition. He agreed the family history suggested such a condition, which through inheritance could manifest itself in a direct descendant, but had found no such condition in Alick Claydon. In his testimony to the court he stated quite categorically that throughout a period

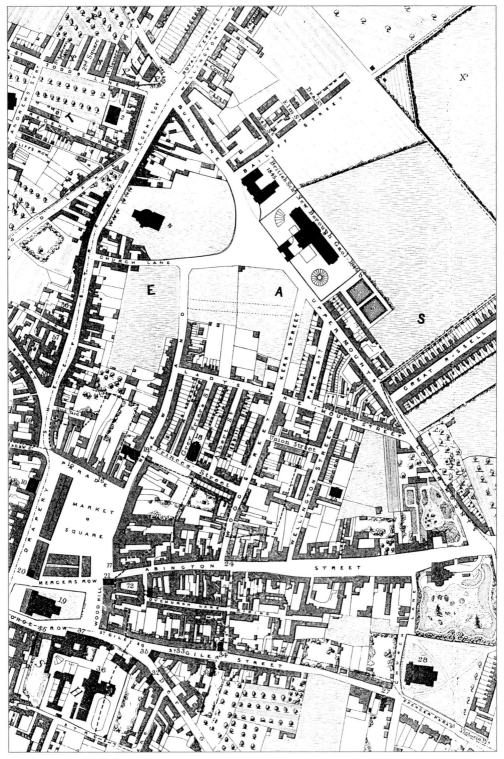

*A map of Northampton showing the location of the prison. (Northampton Library)*

of four months during which Alick had been imprisoned he had carried out a series of examinations. None proved the case for insanity. He was backed up by Dr Lee Cogan, prison surgeon, who while not competent in diagnosing the complete mental condition of his patients, was accepted by the court as being able to identify the early signs of insanity when first found. He agreed totally with Dr Harding's findings and told the jury that at no time had signs of mental incapacity been seen while Alick had been held in prison.

Recognising that his case for insanity had clearly been lost Ryland Adkins, in his closing speech to the jury, asked that they considered a further option: 'On the night of the tragedy the woman had also been drinking, and it was a possibility the jury had to weigh that this fearful crime was the direct and immediate result of a quarrel between the two. If the jury thought so, then it was open to them to return a verdict of manslaughter.'

Manslaughter as a possible verdict had not been raised throughout the trial. For Ryland Adkins to bring it up at that juncture was indicative of desperation and Mr Justice Bigham recognised this immediately. In his summing up he refuted the notion that the killing could have been anything other than murder, and that the jury had only to decide whether or not Alick Claydon did it and whether or not he was sane if he did. They took fully one minute, never leaving the jury box, to return a verdict of guilty.

At eight in the morning on 12 December 1901 he was duly executed. No petition had been raised in his defence, no public clamour for leniency ever demanded and his case was not even taken up by those opposed to capital punishment. He walked to the scaffold that morning as the *Northampton Mercury* put it, 'left by the public, unheeded and unmourned'.

# 11

# AN UNFORTUNATE AFFAIR

## *Kettering, 1912*

Born in Northampton in 1875, Mary Jane Pursglove had lived a somewhat chequered life, constantly on the move, never staying in any one place for long. She had married, at the age of twenty, a serving soldier, but the marriage failed after only six years when he returned with the army to South Africa. At that point, with two children in tow, she changed her name to Pittam and told anyone who asked that her husband had died out there. Living as a widow, she remained in Northampton until the early part of 1902 when she brought her young family to Kettering, eventually moving in with a man named Bell on Carrington Street. How long this relationship lasted is not known but certainly by the time it ended she had a third child, a second daughter, and had reverted to her married name of Pursglove. She and Bell, a railway engine driver, continued to see each other despite the split and when, in 1912, she set up house with 35-year-old Isaac Edward Sewell at 76 Northall Street, it was this old relationship that would be the catalyst for her murder.

Northall Street at that time was considered to be extremely poor housing. Two up, two down terraces forming a narrow thoroughfare that connected Rothwell Road with Rockingham Road, it was among some of the oldest housing in the town and was run down, neglected and populated by families from the bottom end of the social scale. Poverty was very much an accepted norm for most and domestic violence was not uncommon in families struggling to maintain a living in the lowest-paid industrial sector.

When Isaac Sewell met and moved in with Mary, her son, fourteen years old by this time, had already been sent away to a reform school and the family, like many around them, was suffering severe financial hardship. This, coupled with the fact that her eldest daughter, seventeen-year-old Elizabeth, had just given birth to an illegitimate child towards whose upkeep they were expected to pay, meant the pressure placed upon their meagre resources was growing. Unfortunately it is doubtful that Isaac did much to alleviate that pressure. Born in Pytchley, he had moved into the shoe trade that was burgeoning around Kettering because the pay rates were supposedly good.

*Carrington Street, Kettering, 2003. (Author's Collection)*

Unfortunately for Mary, though, Isaac liked a drink and much of his hard-earned wages passed across the bar at the Old White Horse public house. Not that she objected too fiercely. Known as a woman who liked a drink herself, she could hardly have been overly critical, despite the fact it added extra strain to a relationship already beginning to buckle. Almost from the first day the two had come together there was an underlying tension. Mary simply could not stop visiting Bell at Carrington Street.

Isaac, aware from the outset that she had maintained this relationship and in spite of his constant protestations had continued with it, was hugely resentful of the situation. In turn it led to more arguments than those caused by either drink or lack of money. There was no doubt that for him Bell represented a serious risk to what he saw as his own security, and as the weeks passed so the jealousy grew, culminating in an argument on 27 July 1912 when for the first time Isaac threatened physical violence. The sniping at each other continued throughout the day, Mary finally telling him that if he believed her meetings with Bell represented such a serious risk to their relationship he should leave. It was probably no more than a throwaway remark said in the heat of the moment. But to Isaac it was confirmation of the suspicions he had harboured for months, and if there was ever a time Mary had underestimated Isaac's ability to wreak revenge upon her this was it.

*The area around where Northall Street stood before its demolition. (Author's Collection)*

By early evening, not realising how seriously he had taken her comment about leaving the house, she left him alone in the kitchen and went upstairs to lie on the bed. He followed her some few minutes later and lay down beside her. But this was to be no act of contrition. Reaching an arm around her neck he cut her throat from ear to ear. Mary died instantly. Then, quite calmly, he left her where she lay and, locking up the house, walked up the road to the Three Cocks public house, drank two-pennyworth of whisky, then moved on to the Old White Horse. Here he stayed until just after half past nine that night when he was found on the street, drunk, and was arrested by police.

It being July, with long days and light nights, when he left the house both daughters were out. The youngest, six-year-old Gladys, who played with neighbouring children on the street until around eight-thirty that night, was the first to return home. She walked back to the house as her friends were all called in by their parents, to find the doors locked. She knew her mother rarely locked the doors so early and never without letting her know where she had gone. So, somewhat concerned, she went across to a neighbour, Sarah Smith, who walked back with her to try and force a window. None of the sash windows locked easily and Sarah knew that lifting the window at the back of the house was not likely to prove too difficult. Once it was opened she helped Gladys in, told her to find a key to unlock the back door and then stood in the backyard and waited. It was several minutes before she heard the little girl screaming and several more before she got her to open the door. Once inside, a distraught Gladys told her she had gone into an upstairs bedroom looking for the key and found her mother on the bed. Fortunately, because of how her mother lay, she had not seen the extent of the injuries, only the blood which had soaked into the bedclothes; but Sarah, who had to check if Mary was dead, was less fortunate: she saw the full horror of what Isaac Sewell had done.

When Dr Lee arrived at the house a few minutes after the police, at around nine o'clock, Mary had been dead for about two hours. He found two large wounds to her neck, one extending across the right side and severing the windpipe, the second, on the left, much deeper and in his opinion the wound that had killed her. No signs of a struggle were found and so much force had been used that her head had been all but severed. Police, after listening to neighbours tell of the arguments raging inside the house, immediately set out to find Sewell. They did not have to look far. Already in custody for being drunk and disorderly, he was easily identified and left in a cell for the night to sober up.

The following morning, Sunday, he was formally charged with murder. He made no attempt to try and deny or mitigate his involvement: 'I did it about seven o'clock. We were both lying on the bed and I went downstairs and fetched a knife. She was nearly asleep. She never called out. I went out and got drunk. It is all through her going to Bell's.'

The key to the front door was found in his pocket. The back door was already locked before he left the house, and as he wanted to ensure no one entered and found her on the bed he had also locked the front door and taken the key with him. Beyond that he had not thought out the consequences of the killing or its impact on the two daughters; he had just decided to try and drink the problem away.

The inquest was held in the boardroom of Kettering's workhouse on the following Monday. It was a relatively short affair. After evidence as to the body's discovery, the wounds found and Sewell's confession, the jury returned a verdict of wilful murder and the body was released for burial. The funeral took place twenty-four hours later at Kettering cemetery, witnessed by hundreds of people who stood beside the graveside in heavy rain. It was a sad end to an unfortunate life.

For the next three months Sewell languished in prison under no illusion as to the likely outcome of his eventual trial. Guilt had not been in question since the day of his arrest. Bernard Campion on the other hand, appointed by the court to represent him, had other ideas. He needed no reminding of the stakes they played for and his adviser's numerous visits to Sewell in his cell were designed to find the one single fact, or event, that he could use in court to mitigate both the crime and the confession, no easy task given the evidence available to both police and prosecution. But as autumn swept

*Opposite: Kettering cemetery where Mary Jane Pursglove's funeral was held. (Author's Collection)*

away the summer months he believed he had enough to win a courtroom battle. It remained to be seen whether a jury of twelve men would agree with him.

On the morning of 19 October 1912 Isaac Sewell stepped into the dock before Mr Justice Scrutton and pleaded not guilty. The prosecution case was straightforward enough. Witnesses were called to testify to having heard the day-long argument on the day of the murder and to the general drunken state of Sewell after the killing. They also brought to court Katherine Hayden, Mary's mother, who had met him the day before. In her testimony she told the court that he had made a threat against her daughter's life, saying he would kill her, but that she had not taken the threat seriously.

The obvious suggestion was that the killing had been premeditated and the implication that had for the defence was not lost upon Campion. But his strategy had not been to attack or discredit the evidence pointing toward Sewell's guilt but rather to accept it and find mitigating circumstances. He had known from the outset that there was no gain in trying to disprove any of the facts presented by these witnesses. Sewell had confessed, his knife had been used, there was no doubt he had threatened Mary and having the front door key in his pocket proved him to be the last to have left the house. There was no doubt whatsoever that he was Mary's killer. What Campion wanted to show was that at the time of the murder Sewell had suffered a bout of insanity. It was a defence that had been mounted before and if he was to mitigate Sewell's action there was no alternative but to mount it again.

*Kettering, c. 1900, showing how rural the town was in 1912. (Northampton Library)*

*Kettering market place, c. 1900. Northall Street, demolished in the 1960s, once lay just beyond the square. (Northampton Library)*

It transpired that in 1908, four years earlier, Isaac had been involved in a cycling accident. The accident had been severe and had resulted in him being hospitalised for some time, suffering the effects of concussion. This one single incident, claimed Bernard Campion, had rendered him brain-damaged. So much so that from this incident came his eventual lapse into insanity. He brought witness evidence to the court, particularly from Sewell's two brothers, to show that there had been a diminishing of his mental capabilities over the years following the accident. This was backed up by further testimony from colleagues at the shoe factory where Sewell had worked. They insisted that over a four-year period since 1908 he had become far more aggressive with each passing year and over the last twelve months had begun to complain of pains in his head. These stopped him functioning properly and at times had resulted in the work he had carried out having to be re-done. Allied to this was the fact that some members of his family had committed suicide – his father by hanging and an uncle by drowning in a well. According to Bernard Campion there could be no reason other than insanity to explain the actions of Isaac Sewell when he lay on that bed with Mary. Unfortunately the prison doctor, Lee Cogan, disagreed. He told the court that throughout Sewell's incarceration in Northampton prison not once had he exhibited signs of madness. He totally refuted any mental illness suffered by his prisoner and believed him quite sane.

Undeterred by this, Campion, in his address to the jury at the closing of the trial, turned the notion of insanity on its head and declared it only happened the once:

> The question the jury has to consider is the state of mind of the prisoner at the crucial moment when the crime was committed. I have never suggested that at the present moment, or when the man was examined by the prison doctor, he was not sane. I submit that at the moment when the act of extraordinary violence was committed, for some reason or other, his mind was not on its balance, and that it was so far off its balance that he could not control himself. I ask the jury to find a verdict that the prisoner was insane when he committed the crime.

Having called no medical evidence in support of this contention it was an extremely risky path to tread. The prosecution attacked the argument as being unproven in the court and therefore not valid as a defence. They argued strongly that there was only one real reason Isaac Sewell had murdered Mary Ann Pursglove: 'In this case there was the most powerful of motives for the crime. There was no more powerful motive than that of love turned to hate and the attitude of a man toward a woman of whom he was jealous.'

In his summing up of the evidence Mr Justice Scrutton appeared to lean toward the prosecution's assessment of the day's hearing. He reiterated the point that no medical evidence supported the notion of insanity: 'If they [the jury] were satisfied that he [Sewell] knew the nature and quality of the act, though he did it under uncontrollable impulse, they must not find him insane.' The jury disagreed and after an adjournment of forty-five minutes returned a guilty but insane verdict. Isaac Edward Sewell was sent to an asylum for life.

# 12

# A NOT SO PERFECT MARRIAGE

When Frank Copperwaite married his long-time girlfriend Maud at Whitsuntide, 1914, it was supposed to have been a perfect match, a marriage made in heaven as some put it. Maud was only seventeen years old, an innocent in the ways of the world, but the two had known each other since schooldays and Frank, according to his sister, loved every hair on her head. They set up home in rooms at 9 St Edmunds Street, Northampton; he started working in Frederick's boot factory while she settled into her role as housewife. It was the happiest time of their lives and one they would never replicate.

Within days of their wedding world events had begun to shape the future and possibly for the first time in their short lives politics began to impinge upon them in a way they could never have envisaged. Thousands of miles away, in a place neither had probably ever heard of, Austrian Archduke Franz Ferdinand was assassinated while driving through the streets of Sarajevo. Within days newspapers were carrying stories of the gathering clouds of war spreading across the Balkans. Angry and eager for revenge, Austria invaded Serbia in July. Russia supported its Serbian ally, France refused to remain neutral, Germany declared war on the two of them and on 4 August Britain went to war. Its impact upon the two young lovers was to be devastating.

For a whole year they stayed together at St Edmunds Street and watched events unravel in the pages of the national press. Toward the end of 1914 Maud became pregnant, and shortly after Italy entered the war on the side of the allies in 1915 she gave birth to a daughter. But the pressure to join the growing army of men intent on glory was becoming irresistible for Frank. Believing the war would be short, thousands were flocking to the flag. Whether they wanted it or not, both must have realised that the chances of resisting the war reduced with each passing day, and the press trumpeted its virtues. In October 1915 Frank walked into the army's recruitment office in Northampton and joined up.

*St Edmunds Street, Northampton, where Alice and Frank Copperwaite lived in 1914. The terraced street where they set up home was demolished during the 1970s. (Author's Collection)*

A member of the Royal Army Medical Corps, after initial training in England he was sent to the front where he stayed until early 1917. After a spell of leave he was posted to Constantinople and eventually out to Salonica for the remainder of the war. Maud, meanwhile, not satisfied with simply being a housewife, made the decision to become more involved with events abroad and joined the Women's Royal Army Corps at around the same time, arriving in France at the beginning of 1918. It was a decision that would bring scandal and tragedy, in equal measure, to both sides of their family.

In the early part of that year Maud, away from her family for the first time in her life, met another man, a serving soldier. The two embarked upon an affair that was to last for several months. Whether Maud ever viewed it as a serious threat to her marriage is unclear but certainly she became heavily involved and by the summer of 1918 was pregnant. What must have been a desperate time for her was brought to a head by the army who, having no use for a pregnant woman among their ranks, had her discharged and sent back to Northampton. Shame and scandal followed her back and when, in February 1919, she gave birth the baby was immediately put up for adoption. Frank, meanwhile, had no idea of his wife's infidelity and only on his return to England in June 1919 did he discover the awful truth. But by this time the war had taken its toll and Frank was no longer the man who had embarked on his service abroad with so much enthusiasm.

Morose, generally depressed and unable to concentrate on any one thing for more than a few minutes, his health had taken a battering through the war years. News of Maud's pregnancy simply heaped more misery and gloom upon him. Fraught with difficulties from the outset, despite the baby by this time having been successfully adopted, any renewal of their marriage was never going to be easy.

They eventually moved to Ethel Street where they tried to put the past behind them and start a new life. This was easier said than done. Frank's sense of betrayal was like a festering wound and no amount of bandaging was going to make it heal. He became ill, suffering from severe headaches, so severe in fact that having been offered his old job back he had to resign within two days. Concerned for his mental health, he was referred to Northampton's workhouse hospital where he stayed for two weeks.

During this time Maud moved out of their house and took up residence with Frank's married sister, Sarah Marlow, on the Wellingborough road. Perhaps because the marriage was breaking down she made no attempt to return home after Frank's release from hospital at the start of January 1920, leaving him to move back with his mother. The latter, believing strongly that the two of them had to remain married and so must live together, convinced Frank that living with her was no solution at all. If he and Maud were to stand any chance at all of saving their marriage then they had to find rooms to rent together. Frank took some convincing but finally agreed and began the search for accommodation. It was not easy during the winter months, though, and despite his best efforts poor health, lack of financial resources and no firm employment all went toward making it an even harder task. Despondency crept over him, depression returned and he began

*Ethel Street, 2003. (Author's Collection)*

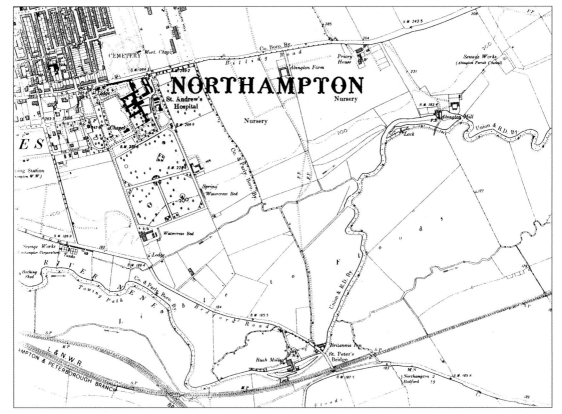

*Map showing Rushmills murder site, c. 1900. (Northampton Library)*

to realise his mother's plan for repairing his marriage had little foundation in reality. So Frank and Maud remained apart, though he did continue to meet her as and when he could.

On 29 January, with prospects of ever resolving the impasse that seemed to strengthen with each passing day growing ever more remote, an event took place that changed irrevocably Frank's view of his wife. A man, a stranger, accosted him in the street late at night as he returned to his mother's house after a visit with Maud. The man was threatening, there was a running fight of sorts, and in the fierce exchange of words that followed it became clear to Frank that this man was involved with his wife – deeply involved. Frightened and unable to defend himself effectively, he retreated to the house on St Edmunds Street with the stranger still in tow. A further scuffle ensued as the man forced his way into the house and it took all of Frank's resolve to eventually evict him. But it had shaped his mind in a way he had never believed possible.

On the following day, 30 January, he arranged to meet Maud along the footpath that ran from the Billing road down to Rushmills at half past seven at night. An unlit area much frequented in summer, it was at that time on a dark winter night an extremely lonely place. Unsuspecting, she turned up on time and at some point in their walk down toward the river Frank took a cut-throat razor from his jacket pocket and slashed her across the throat. So violent was the attack that Maud's head was almost severed and she died instantly. After satisfying himself that she was dead, Frank then removed his overcoat, covered her from the cold and attempted to cut his own throat. Five times he slashed at his neck but despite horrific injuries he failed to kill himself. After several minutes stumbling around in the dark, somewhat disorientated, shivering and drenched in blood, he managed to find his way back on to the Billing road where he met Fred and William Parker. Desperate for help he called out, told them he had killed his wife, asked them to finish the job he had started, then collapsed on the roadway. Fred Parker found Maud's body 150 yards away then ran off to fetch the police. Frank was in a poor way by the time medical assistance arrived but his wounds were not life-threatening.

The inquest opened at the Trumpet Inn, Weston Favell, next day and was promptly adjourned after identification evidence until 16 February. By that time Frank Copperwaite had made a full and complete recovery from his attempted suicide and sat quietly through the proceedings, which returned an expected charge of murder against him. At his next public appearance before magistrates ten days later proceedings were a little more compelling. Interest in the case had been roused through a variety of newspaper reports both local and national, which had brought the public out in their hundreds to see the man responsible for killing his wife. All the public seating was taken within minutes of the pro-ceedings getting under way, with a large body of people, unable to gain

*The Billing road as it looked in 1920 when Frank Copperwaite met Fred and William Parker after the murder. (Northampton Library)*

access, waiting outside on a cold February day. The evidence against Frank was clearly overwhelming. He had never denied the killing; the razor that caused the wounds belonged to him, as did the overcoat found covering her body and he had confessed to the Parker brothers when they stumbled across him. Committing him to trial was, therefore, a foregone conclusion.

The trial, when it opened on 4 June 1920, was equally well attended. But unlike the earlier two proceedings this court appearance had to be handled differently. Frank Copperwaite stood in the dock pleading not guilty in the full knowledge that if the verdict went against him here then he would forfeit his life. He could not have been playing for higher stakes and, despite his feelings at the time of the murder, he had by this time had three months to reappraise the issues surrounding his own actions, and there seems little doubt he wanted the chance to live out his life. This was borne out by the *Northampton Mercury* which reported that compared with his previous appearances 'he was now in much better health'. A short, thick-set man, the bandages had been removed from his neck some weeks prior to the trial, no doubt adding to the sense of well-being their reporter believed he saw. But Copperwaite gave little else away. Nervous, a little agitated, he sat quietly as proceedings began, making only the odd sidelong glance at his defence team, ably led by Sir Ryland Adkins and his assistant, Bernard Campion, the man who had so successfully defended Isaac Sewell eight years earlier.

After hearing evidence of the discovery of the body, the injuries sustained and the circumstances surrounding the night's events, the defence produced a letter. It had been written by Frank Copperwaite on 30 January 1920 and seen by his sister Sarah to have been folded up by him and placed in his trouser pocket during the afternoon of that day, shortly after her arrival at their mother's house:

> God forgive me, as I forgive my wife. Thanking dear old mother for her great kindness to us, but the wife won't help me, and I love her more than words can say, so I am doing the one wrong thing of my life.
>
> A young man, five feet four to five, blue suit, dark hair, dark overcoat, full face, and rather flat nose, thought she belonged to him. Told me to go and leave her with him. Not for mine.
>
> I really think all the people mixed up in this ought to have told me about it. They all knew me personally and that she was my wife.
>
> Good-bye the happy times I longed for.

Clearly, it was a document meant to have been found after both the death of himself and his wife. It contained a very detailed description of a third party, no doubt the man who had accosted him in the street the previous night, and a man he was intent on being able to fully describe. Why? Presumably because this was the man he held responsible for the actions he found himself taking and wanted the world to know it. This, argued Sir Ryland Adkins, was clear evidence of Copperwaite's state of mind at the time he carried out the killing.

To further emphasise the point of just how deranged Frank had become he then produced a series of witnesses, men who had known him toward the end of his four-year army career. These were able to testify to the fact that between January 1917 and December 1918, while serving in Salonica, Frank had suffered from severe bouts of malaria. These had caused long periods of delirium, which even after recovery had left him somewhat taciturn and prone to depression, a condition, Sir Ryland Adkins insisted, he had unfortunately brought back to England on his discharge at the end of the war; a condition that he believed had also resulted in a further decline in mental capability the longer he had remained under such marital pressure. Dr McCandlish, the man who had placed Copperwaite in the workhouse hospital, agreed.

Sir Ryland: Would the fact of another man claiming this man's wife be sufficient to upset his mental balance and render him quite insane?

Dr McCandlish: I do think so.

Sir Ryland: Under such circumstances are you of the opinion that he would not know the nature and quality of the act he was doing, or at that moment, he was doing wrong?

The Judge (interrupting): Did he know he was cutting his wife's throat – that was the nature and quality of the act – and did he know at that moment he was doing wrong?

Dr McCandlish: I think he might not know, my lord.

This short exchange was sufficient to show clearly that Frank Copperwaite was mad. He had probably been in that state since leaving the army one year earlier and his wife's infidelity had simply tipped the scales. To his mind he saw no alternative to the action he took. The sad, tragic poignancy of the whole sorry saga was that he loved the woman he killed far above everything else he had ever had in his life. When Dr William Robson, the final medical witness, took the stand he told the court that he saw Copperwaite four weeks before the killing and was of the opinion that had he been sent away, which had been his suggestion to the family, and had he then not communicated with his wife for a whole year, then none of the events of January would have happened. Because the advice was shunned, what was at the time a suicidal tendency had turned into a homicidal tendency:

Dr Robson (in answer to a question about the letter found): My opinion is that he was then suffering from an obsession that he must kill his wife and that was a recurring obsession. I think that up to the time he committed the crime he had been able to overcome it. The fact of the prisoner covering the dead body of his wife to keep her warm, and the brutality of the crime, were evidences of insanity.

The jury certainly seemed to agree and had no problem, after a twenty-minute adjournment, of finding Frank Cecil Copperwaite to have been quite mad when he carried out the murder. There was to be no June execution.

# 13
# THE PRICE OF LOVE

*Higham Ferrers, 1938*

Albert Hedley Harrison could be described as an upright citizen, a man who had lived his life within the secure shadow of the law, never stepping out beyond its reach and never contravening its covenant with the community in which he lived. Brought up by his parents to respect the police and the office they held, he had always supported the view that laws were meant to free the people around which they were formed, not imprison them. A member of the Salvation Army for much of his life, where these views were commonplace, he had always believed in truth and honesty and no doubt tried hard to incorporate these principles into his daily life.

Born in 1896, he had gone into the shoe industry as a young man and met the love of his life, Mabel, during 1917. A member of a Salvation Army family, she had been a songster accompanying the band around the streets of Chelmsford where she lived with her parents. Within a year the two married and she came with her new husband to live in the then small village of Raunds. Children inevitably followed, two sons, and in 1936, after eighteen years in the same place, they decided to move to 92 Wharf Road, Higham Ferrers. There Albert Hedley Harrison's beliefs were sorely tested.

Both Albert and Mabel worked in shoe factories, he in Raunds, she in Higham Ferrers. Mabel's custom, because her factory was close by, was to come home every day just after midday to eat lunch. From that sprang rumours that she had begun an affair with a married man, Gilbert Talbot, the two meeting at around one each afternoon and on any other occasion when opportunity allowed. Albert was blissfully unaware of these rumours until January 1938. During that month he was either told or had heard the gossip spreading through the Raunds factory. This in turn forced him to ask himself if what he observed as a husband lent credence to what he knew to be speculation. Slowly he began to watch more closely the times his wife went out, where she went and how she appeared on her return. Gradually observation turned to suspicion. He began to realise that subtle changes were taking place within their relationship. Mabel was dressing better, wearing more make-up and going out on her own more than she ever had before. She was organising trips for herself, ostensibly with girlfriends, to places neither would normally go and he found himself constantly checking up on her. In short, he began to accept that quite possibly the rumours were true. However, it made little difference to how he lived his life, burying his head in the sand in the hope that it would all go away. Unfortunately for him it did just the opposite.

During the first week of August 1938 he, Mabel and their twelve-year-old son Keith went off to stay the week with Mabel's sister in Chelmsford. All went well until the Wednesday when Mabel suddenly announced she was off to London. It was an opportunity, she said, to catch up with old friends. There was little Albert could do to stop her going and to his sister-in-law it would have seemed churlish to have even tried. So off she went for the whole day, not returning until well after midnight. Visibly excited the next day, she told Albert she had met several old school friends, had a great time and while there had also seen the changing of the guard. Suspicious, but not sufficiently to cause a row, he listened to her tell the story of her day and then put the whole event to the back of his mind.

On Thursday 18 August, some two weeks later, Kate Talbot, a woman he knew, reminded him of it. After seeking him out in the factory at Raunds she confronted him with the fact that her husband was carrying on an affair with his wife. As proof she knew her husband had met Mabel that same day in London; they had both watched the changing of the guard. Not only that, she went on, but the two had also been meeting secretly every lunchtime near to the Higham Ferrers factory in which they both worked. Then, as if it were irrefutable proof, she produced a packet of condoms found in her husband's pocket. She wanted a showdown with Mabel and she wanted it that night. Albert agreed. The London trip convinced him that the two had met; he needed to know and if it had to be a confrontation then so be it.

Kate duly arrived early that evening at Wharf Road and the inevitable row erupted. She pointedly accused Mabel of having an affair with her husband, cited the evidence and insisted she admit her involvement. Mabel would have none of it. Refusing to acknowledge any association no matter how innocent, she denied ever having met Gilbert Talbot at work let alone in any sort of clandestine meeting place, either in Higham Ferrers or London, and kicked out violently at Albert for even allowing this set-to to take place, striking him repeatedly across his shins. But Kate Talbot was having none of it; she insisted that if Mabel was telling the truth she had to confront Gilbert back at Raunds and tell him to his face. Whether through bravado or sheer stupidity Mabel agreed, and the three of them marched off to the Talbot house, intending to resolve the issue once and for all. Gilbert, though, had heard a whisper of what was to take place that night and done the proverbial runner. The confrontation never took place and despite Albert's best efforts to find him in pubs around Raunds he drew a blank, and the rancorous meeting broke up.

*Newspaper headline of 26 August 1938. (Northampton Mercury)*

But for Albert the damage had been done. Kate Talbot had forced him to face up to his suspicions and accept the truth he had probably always known. That night he and Mabel slept apart.

On the following day, 19 August, Albert decided not to go to work. Instead, after Mabel had left the house he caught a bus to Raunds and asked a good friend, Charles Pettit, to collect his wages for him, timing his return home to miss his wife's lunch break. Still in turmoil over the previous night's events he wanted no confrontation until he felt better able to cope. But an afternoon alone in an empty house did little to lift his spirits. When she finally stepped back through the door at half past five that evening the anger that had festered since dawn finally erupted. He demanded answers to questions that had taken a day to define and sought reassurances that their marriage was still sound. But it appears Mabel was reluctant to offer much by way of comfort despite his best efforts, because for the next hour a row raged between them.

It was at around half past six that night that she finally gave in. Whether she had been worn down by her husband's constant sniping, or simply because she wanted to inflict the decisive blow, no one will ever know, but she suddenly turned on Albert and told him what she thought he wanted to hear. She admitted to the affair. The impact of that admission was devastating. Albert, having sought the knowledge, had no means of handling it. He shouted at her, telling her it had to end. Mabel, having by this time walked into the kitchen, ostensibly to make tea, snapped. Lifting the teapot from the

*Wharf Road, 2003. (Author's Collection)*

draining board she hurled its boiling contents straight at him. He ducked, the water missed, there was a brief skirmish, then she forced her way past him and ran for the stairs.

By now uncontrollable, Albert chased after her and grabbed at her back as she mounted the first stair. He missed, but she fell, striking her eye on the tread and cutting herself badly. Shouting back at him, she turned as he struck out and scratched him viciously across the left side of his face. All sense of discipline lost, he put his hands around her neck and squeezed as the two writhed from one side of the staircase to the other. As Mabel lost consciousness, in one quick movement he pulled a bootlace from his pocket, made a ligature around her throat, and pulled until she was dead.

For several minutes afterwards Albert sat in silence, dazed and shocked by his own actions, his wife's lifeless body staring back at him. Then self-preservation took over. He had arranged to meet Charles Pettit, the friend who had agreed to collect his wages from work, at around eight o'clock on Rushden Bridge. He also knew his younger son Keith had gone to the nearby fair and would not be home until he brought him back at around nine-thirty that night. The elder boy, eighteen-year-old Clifford, was staying away. So, with some three hours before he had to meet young Keith, but only an hour or so before he had to catch the Rushden bus, he set about cleaning up the murder scene.

First, he carried Mabel's corpse upstairs to the small boxroom at the back of the house, checked the body for any signs of life and then, satisfied there were none, wrapped it in a white sheet. Returning to the stairs, which had sustained a fair amount of bloodstaining from her cut eye, he set about trying to clean the carpet, banister and wall. The wall and banister were easy but it took some time to remove sufficient from the stair carpet to disguise the fact that the stains were blood. It was after half past seven before he felt satisfied enough to throw the bloodstained cleaning clothes, along with the clothes he had worn during the killing, into the little boxroom alongside the body. He then nailed the room door shut to prevent any chance discovery during the night.

At twenty minutes past eight on a warm night he and Charles Pettit walked into Rushden's Wheatsheaf hotel. To all intents and purposes it was just two friends having a quiet drink together. Nothing in Albert's appearance betrayed the fact he had been in a fight and nothing in his demeanour suggested to Pettit that his marriage was in any way compromised by the rumours he knew to be sweeping through the shoe factory where they both worked. What was unusual, though, was the fact that Albert took a drink. Known to be an abstemious man, he stepped out of character and drank two glasses of beer then ordered up a quart of whisky, which he took home with him. Pettit noted the event but said nothing to his friend.

At just after half past nine the two men parted. Albert walked on to collect his son from the pre-arranged meeting place outside the fair and took him home. After eating supper together, without apparently ever discussing Mabel despite her non-appearance at the supper table, they both retired to bed. For Albert it was a long and restless night. Awake throughout, he shared his misery with the whisky bottle, draining away the last of it as dawn finally crept through the window. At around half past five in the morning he went downstairs and made himself tea, then sat waiting until half past eight before he dared to call his son down for breakfast. The two of them ate hurriedly and, after packing him off to friends, Albert caught a bus into Rushden, walked into the police station and confessed to his wife's murder.

Inspector Robert Valentine cautioned him at ten o'clock and sat him down for questioning. Albert remained calm, not wanting to appear obdurate or in any way obstructive; he told his story in as dispassionate a way as possible, only insisting that the inspector should go to the house on Wharf Road as soon as his statement had been concluded, because his son would be returning for dinner at around midday. At this point he took a key from his pocket and passed it across the table. Taking it, Inspector Valentine quickly assembled a team consisting of himself, Detective Sergeant Mencock and a local GP, Dr Muriset.

They all arrived at the house an hour later and let themselves in by the back door. At the top of the stairs they found the sealed boxroom just as Albert had told them they would, and after forcing it open found the body of Mabel Harrison. She was wrapped tightly in the bloodstained white sheet; discarded

*The Wheatsheaf Hotel, Rushden, where Albert Hedley Harrison bought a quarter bottle of whisky after the murder of his wife. (Author's Collection)*

*High Street, Higham Ferrers, 2003. (Author's Collection)*

and also bloodstained, pieces of clothing littered much of the floor, these obviously used during his frenzied attempt at cleaning the scene. Despite Albert's desperate efforts they also found clear impressions of footmarks still on the stair wall indicating exactly where the main struggle had taken place and just how violent it had been. Lifting the still-wet stair carpet revealed heavy staining on the floorboards beneath, and further forensic testing found similar stains adhering to the banister, the jamb of the kitchen door, the skirting board at the bottom of the stairs and around the door between the kitchen and pantry. The cleaning, done in a hurry, had been largely ineffectual.

Satisfied they now had a good indication of just how violent the fight on the stairs had been, the police then turned their attention to the descriptive detail of Albert's confession to the killing – in particular, his reasoning as to motive at the time that he had strangled her. Did his assertion that the murder had been committed while in a fit of uncontrollable rage hold true to the facts as found, or could a different interpretation be attributed to them?

A cursory medical examination by Dr Muriset did little more than confirm that death had been some twelve hours earlier and due to asphyxiation. They had to wait until two in the afternoon for the arrival of Dr Webster, head of Birmingham Science Laboratory, to obtain a more detailed assessment of the circumstances surrounding Mabel Harrison's murder. He was able to confirm that Albert had not lied about strangling his wife, that a ligature had indeed been used and was found still wrapped around her neck, but that death had been due entirely to manual strangulation. The ligature, it appeared, had been no more than window dressing; by the time it had been applied Mabel was already dead. So, quite possibly Albert's version of events could have had the ring of truth about it.

On 1 September 1938 he was brought from Bedford prison, where he had been languishing since that August confession, to a town bedecked with flags. Higham Ferrers had been celebrating a hospital carnival. As the *Northampton Mercury* reported it: 'Outside the tiny Town Hall there waved, with remarkable incongruity to the proceedings inside, gay flags and bunting.' Whether Albert Harrison noted the irony of the situation is not known but it is probably safe to say his mind would have been on other things. Arriving half an hour before proceedings began he sat in calm consultation with his defence counsel until the six magistrates took their seats and indicated to the prosecution to open their case. There was nothing contentious in their opening address. It was, they claimed, a clear-cut case of murder and Albert Harrison had put his name to a statement in which he confessed to the killing of his wife. Their intention was simple enough, to prove the accuracy of that confession, and they certainly had sufficient forensic evidence to support their argument.

The defence on the other hand had arrived in court to argue not innocence – there was little value in trying to disprove so well-defined a document as a confession – but manslaughter. Their contention from the outset was that Albert Harrison had suffered severe provocation, enough to have instigated the assault and the intention of killing his wife. But, they suggested strongly as the hearing drew to a close, that because Albert Harrison had neither history nor reputation against him it could not be argued that he had simply become a murderer overnight. No evidence was produced in court that would have supported that notion; in fact, the defence insisted, enough evidence existed to show that he loved his wife deeply and could never have committed the murder had he been in his right mind at the time:

After the wife had taunted the husband with her desire to go with this man Talbot, it was in the passion of the quarrel that this act was done.

I suggest it was done in the heat of the moment and that it is manslaughter.

There is no question of design. The body was put in the room so that a child should not come upon it. I do say that the killing in the heat of the moment, inspired by the wife's conduct, is manslaughter and not murder.

Mr Granville-Smith, who made that plea, gave a strong impression he believed implicitly in every word of it. Obviously the prosecuting counsel did not. They had produced what they considered to be serious incriminating evidence. Two key pieces of evidence brought into court had, they argued,

*Higham Ferrers' Town Hall where Albert Hedley Harrison first appeared in 1938.*
*(Author's Collection)*

supported their contention that Albert had committed a premeditated murder. Firstly the testimony of a previously unheard witness, Harold Rowthorn, a neighbour of the Harrisons, who had told the court that he had been approached by Mabel on the day of her killing at around one in the afternoon. She had arrived home for lunch and the two met outside the house on Wharf Road. She needed his expertise in the water softening industry. Whether she intended to buy some sort of equipment that his firm supplied was unclear, but either way she had arranged that he call around that same evening at six for them to discuss it. Minutes before the designated hour Albert Harrison knocked on his door and told him not to bother, that he and his wife had to go out and would he call on the following Saturday. Why? Because, argued the prosecution, Albert had planned to kill his wife and could not afford any kind of interruption that would have distracted him from his purpose.

The second piece of evidence was the ligature. It had been proved to come from one of his son's football boots, the pair always kept together outside the house. To have unlaced one boot only and kept that lace in a trouser pocket suggested a conscious and calculated decision to arm himself with the means to strangle his wife. The fact it had not been responsible for her death was, they insisted, irrelevant, because it had been used with that intent in mind. It was a logical argument. Police had known since the discovery of the son's boots that Harrison could not have left Mabel half dead while he ran outside to find a suitable ligature. The fact that there had been only one lace taken just gave more credence to the claim that some deliberation or planning had gone into killing her. After hearing this debate the magistrates erred on the side of caution and Harrison was duly committed for trial at the October assizes.

Here there was to be a very different outcome. When Mr Justice Oliver took his seat at ten on the morning of 21 October 1938 crowds had been gathering for over an hour and a half. The rush to find seating in the public galleries had filled the court to capacity. But from the outset it was clear this was not to be a trial in the expected sense. After pleading not guilty to the charge of murder, Albert Harrison became the centre of fierce legal debate and argument from the moment the prosecuting counsel took to his feet.

The contention, as at the earlier magistrates' hearing, continued to revolve around the notion that a degree of premeditation had gone into the killing, but with one very notable difference. Mr Healy, acting for the crown, told the jury that it was his ardent belief that if they accepted the idea that Harrison had killed not through guile or design but had done so under intolerable provocation, they should consider one key aspect of the case not raised before. Provocation could only have happened while the two were in the kitchen and after Mabel Harrison had hurled boiling water at him. After that incident, he argued strongly, there had to have been a pause, albeit short, after which she ran for the stairs. If provocation had been the instigator of the killing it would have taken place in the kitchen, not at the bottom of the stairs. Once there, provocation had passed and been replaced by self-control: enough self-control to elicit murder.

Mr Justice Oliver stopped the proceedings at that juncture and had the jury taken out. He had recognised that if the defence tried to mitigate the killing by arguing provocation they would lose. As he pointed out there could only be one defence for murder – self-defence. Provocation, while relevant, was not a reasonable, accepted defence in law. There followed a series of legal arguments and debates around the issue raised. Finally Mr Justice Oliver, addressing the prosecution team, asked them if they had accepted the statement Harrison had made immediately after his caution in Rushden police station:

Mr Justice Oliver (to prosecuting counsel): Have you any evidence that this statement [the prisoner's] is not true in every particular?

Mr Healy: No, my lord.

Mr Justice Oliver: You would be prepared to accept it?

Mr Healy: I think that is so, my lord.

Mr Justice Oliver: In this circumstance do you think any jury would be at all likely, under proper direction – if this man received provocation sufficient to deprive an average reasonable man of his self-control – to find a verdict of murder?

Mr Healy: It would be open to the jury. . . .

But Mr Justice Oliver decided that it was not going to be put before the jury as a murder. Once he knew that the prosecution had accepted Harrison's statement made hours after the killing and to all intents and purposes a signed confession, there could be no argument of premeditation. Harrison had never claimed to plan his wife's death; he had always insisted it was a reaction to a situation in which he had found himself.

Mr Justice Oliver (to the prosecution): He must be guilty in any case of manslaughter, and I would consider a plea of guilty to manslaughter sufficient in this case if you did.

Mr Healy: I would certainly accept it.

Whether or not it was with some reservation made little difference – the judge's strong recommendation ensured it happened – but Albert Harrison rose to his feet a second time and changed his plea in accordance with the court's wishes, to guilty.

At that point Mr Norman Birkett, KC, acting on behalf of the prisoner who had now accepted his guilt, and before a jury, newly returned to the court, made one of the most powerful and eloquent speeches ever made in defence of a guilty man. Getting to his feet he spoke of Albert Harrison's exemplary character, a man considered kind, tolerant, loving and forgiving by all who knew him. He cited the investigating police officers' report, which had not been aired in court, that told of a failure during their investigation of the crime to uncover any history of previous violence and of how the police had come to regard their prisoner 'as a sober, inoffensive, peaceable man'. As far as provocation went, Birkett asserted: 'It had extended over many years and had it been necessary it would have been possible here to-day to indicate how from day to day, from year to year, this man endeavoured, with nobility of character, to save his wife, to save his home, and to save his children.' He went on to analyse the crime and ended with a direct plea to the judge to return a lenient sentence on a man who had shown neither malice nor evil.

According to the *Northampton Mercury*'s later report it had been a powerful and moving address. The judge agreed and Albert Hedley Harrison was sentenced to only three years' imprisonment.

# 14

# THE MYSTERY OF
# WEST LODGE

*Ashton, 1952*

The picturesque village of Ashton lies in the north-eastern corner of Northamptonshire, sandwiched between the market town of Oundle, some two miles west, and the small village of Polebrook, a mile to the east. A key part of the Ashton Wold estate and situated a mile from its heart, it was originally no more than a small hamlet which was rebuilt by the Hon. Charles Rothschild in 1900 to exacting standards. The old, dilapidated houses were demolished and a total of thirty-two thatched houses constructed in their place. A refusal to allow further expansion over the years has ensured this number has remained constant. At the time of the rebuild the architects responsible for their design were given the freedom to incorporate into each house as much of the new twentieth-century technology as was available. This resulted in an open design layout that created a village where each household had access to its own large garden, a piped water supply, electricity and a bath plumbed into the house. It was innovative in its day and seen by many as the flagship for future similar construction programmes.

Into these houses were brought a range of skilled farm workers ranging from farm managers to general labourers, and all employed to work on the land managed by the various farms either within Ashton itself or within the boundary of the estate's 5,000 acres of arable land. Ashton Wold, the name by which the estate was known, and still is, remained a tiny hamlet of cottages separated from the village proper and bisected by a single-track road out of Ashton's centre that ran on to the Mansion House which Charles Rothschild had constructed at the same time to house his family. Along that same stretch of road two houses, one on the eastern boundary and one on the western boundary, were also built to control access in and out of the estate. Always known locally as East and West Lodge, or Gate House, these houses were of necessity isolated.

For 66-year-old George Peach that very isolation was attractive. A self-sufficient, competent man with a variety of self-taught trade skills, it held less fear for him than it would for most. He and his wife Lillian had moved into

*Newspaper headline from October 1952 with a detailed report of the discovery of the bodies of George and Lillian Peach. (Northampton Mercury)*

East Lodge in the spring of 1946. Keen gardeners, which suited the needs of the house, they had quickly settled into village routine and estate life – quite an accomplishment after a lifetime living in a tiny cottage in the picturesque village of neighbouring Fotheringay where George had been working as a groom. At Ashton, while those abilities were still needed, it was his ad hoc skills as a general handyman that were in greater demand. A year later he had incorporated being a part-time gamekeeper into the role, and over the next five years gradually widened his responsibilities even further, until by 1951 his handyman skills had been replaced by those of part-time cowman.

Cattle were an integral part of the estate's successful farming policy. Over the years a substantial investment had been made in the creation of a much-envied pedigree herd of cows. Prestige followed if the best of these won rosettes at the various agricultural shows around the country. In turn that meant those involved with their handling were often sent away to supervise the grooming and showing, which created the opening for George. These enforced absences affected the day-to-day routines on the estate and so George, with his wide experience of cattle, was a natural to fill the gaps they left behind them.

*West Lodge, Ashton, in which George and Lillian Peach were found murdered in October 1952. (Author's Collection)*

Recognising his growing importance and realising the need for George to be nearer the dairy herd, which was generally to be found at the western end of the estate, the farm manager John Dockraye organised for the Peaches to be moved from East to West Lodge. Situated as it was some half a mile from the village's northern edge, it better facilitated his involvement with milking. Mill Farm, where the cattle returned each morning and night, was only three-quarters of a mile from the house, which meant it was simple for all involved to stay in regular contact.

George appeared to have expressed no undue concerns about the move, he and Lillian settling in as they had at East Lodge with reasonable ease. Throughout the summer of 1952 he covered for those taking sick days or holidays and in October stepped in as replacement for the two-man team of head herdsman Francis Mahoney and stockman Frederick Hadman on a more full-time basis. Both had been sent to the Olympia Show in London which ran for over a week. This meant George's days would be longer, as would his working week, but there was the compensation of extra pay and George rarely turned down overtime opportunities. After a shared responsibility with the regular cowman John Oliver the period finally drew to a close on Friday 24 October and George left work at his usual time of around six in the evening. That same day both men had expressed concern about a particular cow due to calve, and as he left Mill Farm to cycle back through the village he told Oliver to fetch him in the night if needed. It was the last time George Peach was seen alive.

At ten o'clock on the following Saturday morning 23-year-old Laurence Wright, the local butcher boy, brought his delivery van into Ashton village. He was later than usual after a sleepless night because of toothache and had detoured to see a dentist in Oundle. Normally he would have stopped off at the Slaters', who ran the village pub, and shared a coffee. But not feeling at all well he had driven straight to his first call of the morning, West Lodge.

Lillian Peach was a regular customer and so he knew the house well. Driving up to the front of the house, he turned the van around to save himself time and, taking his delivery basket from the back, walked through the open front gate, across the front garden and around to the back door. Unusual for the Peaches, he noticed as he passed by the lounge window that the curtains were still drawn. Nevertheless, expecting to find Mrs Peach cleaning the kitchen fire grate he turned the corner to the back of the house and grabbed hold of the door handle. The door was still locked. Peering in through the kitchen windows – the curtains here had not been drawn – he could see no sign of life so gave the door a couple of loud knocks.

When that brought no response Laurence did what he had done on other occasions when the Peaches had had to go out; he looked for the dinner plate Mrs Peach always left in the lavatory. The back door stood inside a narrow porch, kitchen door on the right, pantry in the middle and lavatory door on the left. It had been her practice since moving into the lodge a year before to leave this plate on a stool or chair with the money for her order beside it if she was not going to be there when he called, but not that morning. If it had

*Mill Farm, where George Peach had been working on the day of the murders. (Author's Collection)*

not been a Saturday and the meat intended for Sunday's dinner Lawrence would probably have taken it back to the shop. But because it was a weekend the joint would have to go to a neighbour to be passed on. The nearest house to West Lodge, he decided, was the pub. So without further ado he put the meat back into his basket and set off along the back garden toward his waiting van. As he reached the top corner of the house he noticed what he at first thought to be an open window. Intending to try and rouse anybody in the house he strained to push his head through the gap before realising it was only the top window section of the house coalbunker. Its significance would only be realised much later.

Frank Slater, landlord of the Three Horseshoes (as it was in 1952), watched the van pull up outside and met Laurence as he brought the Peaches' meat into the bar. He had known since his wife had returned from Mill Farm at nine that morning that George had not turned up for work. Listening to the story of closed curtains and no one around gave him some cause for concern. He knew George to be a dependable, conscientious man, not the type to be ill without letting the estate office know. If the house was still in darkness he supposed that had to mean both were ill, and if Lillian had not been able to answer the door that illness had to be serious. Leaving the meat in the pub kitchen and sending Laurence on his way, he took a walk across the green to Chapel Farm. Placed as it was in the centre of Ashton it was the ideal location for the estate office, and the place he knew he would find John Dockraye. After telling him the butcher boy's tale and expressing his own concerns, Dockraye asked his secretary to take the estate car and drive Slater up to the lodge to find out just what was going on.

They arrived at a little after half past ten. The house was just as Laurence had described it, curtains still closed and back door locked. Standing in the

*The Three Horseshoes at Ashton village, where Frank Slater lived. Today it is called the Chequered Skipper. (Author's Collection)*

garden, Slater shouted up at the back bedroom trying to elicit some sort of response. When that failed he walked around to the front of the house and tried the door. To his great surprise it opened. He said later:

> The house was dark with the curtains drawn. I called Mr Peach again and getting no reply went upstairs. At the top of the stairs the door to one bedroom was slightly open and I went in. Mrs Peach, whom I recognised, was lying on the bed breathing heavily. I saw that all around her throat was covered in blood. The bedclothes were thrown back down to her feet. She was pretty far gone and beyond speech. I did not put the light on then. I came out and looked in the front bedroom which I saw was empty and the bed had not been slept in. I did not try the back bedroom.

Perhaps, understandably, his initial reaction was that Lillian Peach had cut her throat. The fact she had not acknowledged his presence convinced him she was unconscious and without some sort of urgent medical care, which he knew was beyond his own capabilities, her chances of survival were poor. Running back down the stairs to the waiting car the two of them sped off to Chapel Farm. There then followed some hurried discussion in the farm office about what to do before it was finally decided that while the office notified the police and found a doctor Slater, along with the estate chauffeur Albert Christopher who had walked in on the conversation, would go back to the house. Christopher had a degree of first-aid knowledge, leastways more than anyone else in the office, and was happy enough to try and help.

*The road through Ashton village looking toward West Lodge. (Author's Collection)*

Once back at the house it was Christopher who realised that Lillian Peach, far from having cut her throat, had been attacked with some sort of blunt instrument and beaten repeatedly about her head. He could clearly see the marks left across the top of her head, all of which had obviously been bleeding for some considerable time, causing the blood to congeal around her neck. How much blood had been lost was difficult to judge. Lying as she was he could also clearly see she had made some sort of attempt at getting out of the bed. All the bedding had been pulled back from her right shoulder to her feet, which were still covered, indicating perhaps that she had intended to get up then been prevented from doing so. Taking hold of the sheets he pulled them back over her in an attempt to raise her body temperature. The two men then went to find George Peach.

The staircase ran down to meet the front door in a short hallway. From the top step Lillian Peach's bedroom was on the immediate right and looked out over the side of the house. Its door faced on to a short corridor, no more than 5 feet square, off which were two other doors. One opened into a room over the front of the house, the room Frank Slater had already entered and found empty, the other into a room at the back of the house. This second door was the obvious choice. Gingerly turning the knob, they found it locked. Calling out but receiving no reply, Christopher then charged it with his shoulder and forced a way in.

George Peach lay in a single bed, the blankets tightly tucked in around him and pulled up to just beneath his chin. He was dead and had been bludgeoned with some sort of blunt instrument, but not in the same sort of frenzied attack that had been made on his wife. The blows across the top of his head were less numerous. Blood splattered the walls either side of where he lay, sprayed up across the bed head and formed a pattern across the door through which they had just burst in. Without the enormous blood loss, much of which had pooled under the bed, he would have given the appearance of a man asleep. From their vantage point just inside the door the two men could see no signs of a struggle. In the sparsely furnished room, the bed faced the door and a small

*View of the pantry window through which police believed the killer had entered the house. (Author's Collection)*

wooden chair stood to the right, upon which rested the clothes George Peach had taken off the night before. The only other feature in the room was an open fireplace along the back wall. Glancing down, Christopher checked the door lock and found the key missing.

Just as they stepped back on to the landing Dr Ivor Spurrell, who had been called in from his Oundle surgery, shouted up to them and Slater met him on the stairs. Leaving George where he lay he focused his attention on Lillian, but like Christopher before him struggled to find anything he could do to help her. As he attended the injured woman he was joined by Inspector Harold Peel who had received a telephone call from Ashton's estate office at around the same time as the doctor. Taking charge, he sent Christopher and Slater back to the estate office to call an ambulance, then spent the next twenty minutes or so assisting the doctor in his attempts to stabilise Mrs Peach until it arrived.

Once discharged of their patient the doctor and Inspector Peel went into the back room to examine George's body in greater detail. The inspector's later statement, which had been made within hours of his arrival, accurately described the crime scene as he saw it that morning.

> I saw that the bed clothing was not disarranged and was up to the level of his chin, his head is turned to the left side. There was a large quantity of congealed blood on the pillow by the left side of the head. There was considerable blood splashes on the ceiling above the bed and on the wall on the door side of the room. The opposite direction to which the head was facing. The marks on the wall appeared to have been caused by some instrument with wet blood on it being moved up and or down sharply causing the blood to splash on the walls. Dr Spurrell moved the head slightly to the normal position which then revealed severe wounds to the left temple region and jaw. He then pulled the bedclothes back as far as the pelvis and felt the arms. He informed me that in his opinion death had occurred some 5 hours previously at least.

The weapon he referred to was quickly identified as a hammer; exactly what type of hammer at that stage of the investigation was undetermined, but the significance of the window Laurence Wright had found ajar led Inspector Peel to believe it had come from the Peaches' coalbunker and had been used in both attacks. Dr Spurrell, having seen the wounds sustained by Lillian Peach while he attempted to dress them, and then viewed George Peach's body post-mortem, was of like mind. How or why was a question for later.

Inspector Peel's description of how he had found West Lodge that morning would go a long way to answering those questions, as he was only too keenly aware. With that in mind, and conscious his presence at the scene had not been the first, he set about examining the place with a discriminating eye. The house consisted of three upper rooms, a pantry adjacent to the kitchen from which a door opened into an almost semi-circular lounge, and a hallway, which housed the staircase and a door to the bathroom. In his statement he recorded that all the downstairs rooms were tidy. Nothing in his opinion had been disturbed nor, as far as he could ascertain, had any type of search been carried out. The back door was securely locked, with its key still in the door. A second key to a mortice lock ('probably the front door') lay in the centre of the kitchen table. In the pantry, which was packed with all manner of kitchen items completely filling its shelves and spreading across part of the stone floor, a pane of glass appeared to have been removed from the window and the ratchet arm was unfastened.

Above everything else that took place in the investigation to solve the Peaches' murder it was this one simple fact, the broken window, that dominated police thinking and dictated the direction in which it would go. This narrow window, some 5 feet off the ground, consisted of twelve small, leaded panes of glass. The pane at the bottom right-hand side had been removed but neither this, nor any broken shards to indicate it had been smashed during its removal, were ever found. From this initial report of Inspector Peel's it was hypothesised that the house must have been broken into at some point during the night. Forensic examination later that morning assisted that belief when it revealed a single fingerprint found around the area of the window ledge. It was a partial print but everyone was confident that enough detail existed to confirm any match found.

By early evening pathologist James Webster of the Birmingham Forensic Laboratory had also completed his initial examination of George Peach and had been able to confirm to police that the injuries he had sustained, believed to have been inflicted by a hammer, were caused by exactly that. Some half a dozen blows in his case, all delivered to the head, and he had undoubtedly died while asleep: 'In Peach's case while the main injuries indicate a blunt or round headed instrument such as a hammer . . . there was a small injury on the outer end of the left eyebrow which was of a nature of a blunt stab and indicates some kind of spike or pointed contraption on the weapon.'

This stabbing injury at first appeared unusual. But if the hammer in question had been a coal hammer, as the open bunker window had suggested, then it would have been a hammer with a spiked end. In 1952 coal hammers were a necessity, every house owned one, and invariably they were kept with the coal and used to break up the larger pieces before bringing the coal to the fire. The obvious fact was that whoever had killed the Peaches had taken their hammer, possibly to facilitate breaking in, but had then used it to kill. This seemed perfectly plausible and was accepted by everyone on the investigation team. Lillian Peach's death at quarter to eight that same evening created a second opportunity for Professor Webster to add a little more detail to the burgeoning theory.

In the meantime Oundle police, perhaps feeling out of their depth and unaccustomed to murder of this type, particularly a double killing, called in Scotland Yard and handed over control of their investigation. The decision in fact had been taken as early as two in the afternoon, well in advance of the second death; and while they were briefing the growing number of press men Inspector Wilfred Tarr and Detective Sergeant Albert Foster were boarding a train in London bound for Northamptonshire.

Their arrival in Northampton at eleven that night precipitated a meeting in Oundle that lasted into the early hours of Sunday morning. During the meeting they were brought up to date with the details of the case and the evolving theory of it being a break-in that had gone wrong. Inspector Tarr accepted the logic behind the speculation and spent the rest of the night in a local hotel.

On Sunday morning the Peaches' son Jack and his wife Joan, having been located in Staines on Saturday night, were brought to Ashton. At that meeting it had been the police intention to try and obtain confirmation that a robbery had taken place. By this juncture they had only been able to surmise that cash had been stolen. No money, despite George Peach having been paid before he had left work on the Friday, had been found anywhere in the house. Police wanted the couple to confirm whether or not, as local rumour insisted, there was any significant amount of money hidden away in some secret location within one of the rooms of the house. A post office savings book and a bank book, neither of which contained any money, tended to suggest some truth to the rumour. But Jack, who had never lived at West Lodge though he had been a regular visitor, told the Scotland Yard officers that to his knowledge his parents had never had money beyond that which they used on a weekly basis. Citing his father's low pay, which he believed to have been in the region of £6 or £7 a week, he drew the obvious conclusion that savings had never been an option. Joan Peach, who had lived with her in-laws for several months between September 1950 and May 1952, agreed. Whatever money did exist, she insisted, had always been kept by Lillian Peach in a handbag in the bedroom in which her body had been found, though never any significant amount.

This went part-way toward the confirmation they sought. The handbag was still where it had been left but no money had been found inside. Neither had any been found among George Peach's belongings, not even loose change, yet by the time of that meeting they knew he had been paid a week's wage of £9 13s 6d before he had left Mill Farm at around six on the Friday night. Overtime payments for his cover with the dairy herd had obviously inflated the normal weekly amount. If, as the couple said, savings were not common practice in the house, which scotched local rumour, it still left this wage packet and whatever Lillian Peach had kept in her bedroom to be accounted for. After the meeting everyone involved agreed that despite the lack of significant cash the robbery theory was still the more likely and all readily accepted it as the motive for the murders.

Twenty-four hours later, on Monday 27 October, Professor Webster carried out a full post-mortem on both bodies. His findings corroborated his earlier assessment of the injuries, including the use of a hammer as a murder weapon and George having been murdered as he slept. Lillian Peach, he was able to show, had put up fierce resistance. The assault on her had been, as Albert Christopher had postulated, while she remained on the bed. The attacker had struck her thirty-one times, most of the blows centred around her head, at one stage grabbing her left arm to hold it away from her as he struck, judging by her bruises. He had also moved around the room because the pattern and shape of the blows indicated they had not all been delivered from one point: no easy feat when the woman had slept in a normal size double bed. Significantly, Webster had also found similar stab wounds around her neck to those on her husband, caused he believed by the spiked end of a coal or tiler's hammer. After concluding these examinations he had then carried out a calculation based around the amount of secreted urine found in George Peach's bladder. This enabled him to reach a reasonably accurate time of death. In conclusion he reported that in his expert opinion the man had died at around one in the morning.

With no hammer found in the Peaches' coalbunker, logic dictated the hammer used had to be theirs. In turn that gave credence to the idea that it had not been a planned crime. Whoever had entered the Peaches' house that night had not arrived equipped with a weapon. Robbing the coalbunker first smacked of an opportunist theft gone wrong. Inspector Tarr set its discovery as a priority and to that end drafted in more police officers and widened the search area.

While this was ongoing the door-to-door enquiry team, which had discovered a substantial amount of information about people's movements in and around Ashton on the night of the murder, had moved from the immediate area into Polebrook village. From there, aware of the camp for foreign nationals based at Polebrook's Second World War airfield, they had visited the camp to begin interviewing the itinerant workforce late on the afternoon of Monday 27th. Here they found their first serious suspect.

The camp consisted of a series of huts left from the Second World War and occupied by a thirty-six-strong workforce of foreign nationals. All men, they worked as casual labourers wherever jobs were available: some at Ashton Wold in the gardens, others on the land if sufficient work existed and some for the American airforce at Molesworth. While questioning personnel at the site it became clear to police that one man, 27-year-old Nikolaus Skoropei, appeared to be the only individual to have left the camp during Friday night and not returned before midnight. His absence had been noted because of one main fact: he had borrowed a bicycle from a fellow Ukrainian on the pretext of having to visit Oundle police station. A prerequisite of all foreign nationals during their stay in the UK at that time was that they register with the local

*The Oundle to Polebrook village road. (Author's Collection)*

police and keep them informed of any changes to their circumstances. So his request to borrow the bike was not unusual. His failure to return to the camp at a reasonable time, however, certainly was. Bicycles were a much-coveted means of transport. Concerned for its safe return, the man making the loan had sat up much of the night watching for Skoropei's arrival, and as the two men shared the same living accommodation it was reasonable that he would have noted the time his bicycle came back. It was a little after six.

When interviewed, Skoropei, who had lived in England since July 1948, told officers he had borrowed the bicycle just to get him into Oundle for a night out. His claim to have visited a police station had been a lie as no one would have loaned him a bicycle if they had known his true purpose. In Oundle he claimed he had visited most of the pubs along the main street, and then at around nine he had followed a group of men dressed in dinner jackets to see where they were going. When he saw them all walk into the Drill Hall and heard music coming from an upstairs room he bought a ticket for 3s from a man at the door and went inside. According to his statement he stayed at the dance until it finished at a little after one o'clock in the morning, then walked back to the camp. He explained the chain on the bicycle had broken and so he had been forced to push it rather than ride, but he could not explain why the three-mile walk had taken him five hours.

He was telling the truth about the bike; its owner confirmed the broken chain. But the investigating team refused to accept that as an excuse to have taken so long to walk such a short distance. They all knew that the walk back from Oundle would have taken him past Mill Farm and the bottom of Ashton village. Any detour and he could so easily have been outside the Peach house. Inspector Tarr had all the clothes seized that Skoropei claimed to have worn

*Oundle as it looks in 2003. (Author's Collection)*

on the night and sent them for forensic testing. He also instigated a search of his belongings. It revealed little by way of money but did find a hammer. That too went off for scientific testing.

Diligent police work over the next few days succeeded in tracing almost everyone who had attended the dance. This in turn produced a list of individuals able to identify and corroborate most of what the Ukrainian had said in his statement, but no one could positively state what time he had left. What most could testify to, however, was the amount of money he had spent over the bar. Methodically, police then began to piece together his night's spending and were reasonably sure at the end of the exercise that most of what he had been paid prior to leaving the camp had been spent. If robbery had been the motive at West Lodge then Skoropei could have been the man responsible. But they all knew there were other niggling doubts, particularly in the case of his clothes. Lillian Peach had been so violently attacked that the perpetrator must have sustained considerable bloodstaining to his person – impossible not to have with the amount of blood found splattered across the bedroom walls. Yet all knew at the time they had taken the man's clothing away that no such staining could be seen on any of the items.

Nevertheless, when the report came back to Inspector Tarr's desk it showed the jacket, trousers and shirt Skoropei had worn that night had all tested positive. Blood was found on all those items and it matched the Peaches' blood type. However there was not enough of it and medical records showed that not only did the Ukrainian have a tendency to suffer nosebleeds, but that he and the Peaches shared the same blood group. What finally took him off the suspect list, though, came from fingerprint analysis. His prints had been routinely taken and checked against the print found in the pantry – it failed to match. Interest quickly waned and Skoropei returned to relative obscurity.

On 31 October, seven days after the murders and twenty-four hours after the Skoropei interviews, the funeral service for George and Lillian Peach was held at the picturesque little church at Fotheringay. The coffins were borne into the church draped in the Union flag, an honour bestowed on both victims by the British Legion who wished to honour George's First World War service. They were then taken outside and buried in the church's cemetery within sight of the tiny cottage that had been their home up until the move in 1946 to Ashton. Hundreds attended despite the family's wish that it remain a quiet, private affair, though most stood out on the street and watched from a discreet distance.

As Inspector Tarr travelled back to Oundle that night, no doubt wrestling with the lack of progress at the end of the first week of his investigation, he must also have been conscious of the fact that with each passing day his chances of success diminished even further. By this time the police had checked the fingerprint records of all known housebreakers in and around the area without any positive result. They had also failed to locate the missing bedroom key, still not resolved the mystery of the missing pane of glass and, despite numerous searches, not discovered the whereabouts of the hammer responsible for the two deaths. They desperately needed a breakthrough.

It came on the following Saturday, 1 November. Florence Marsh, wife of the head gamekeeper, was searching her garden for a ring lost by her young daughter and found a hammer. What was more, the hammer had what appeared to be human hair adhering to the head. It lay in a vegetable patch some 9 feet from a wall that screened the garden from the main street, and opposite the village green and pub. Measuring 13 inches top to bottom, the hammer was presumed to be that missing from the Peaches' coalbunker. However, it had no spiked or pointed end; it was a simple claw hammer. Three days later forensic testing had proved that the hair belonged to George Peach. In the light of such overwhelming evidence Professor Webster reassessed his earlier statement in relation to the stab wounds found on the bodies and the weapon that had caused them, deciding the claw of the hammer found could well have been responsible. So at last they had the murder weapon. Just how it had come to be found after seven days in an Ashton garden was not discussed, at least not in public.

Inspector Tarr, with his first piece of real, tangible evidence, simply needed to prove its provenance. Unquestionably it had been used to murder George Peach but had it come from his coalbunker? To be certain, he had all the coal hawkers that had delivered coal to West Lodge at any stage over the past year brought into Oundle police station. There were four of them and each in turn

*The Drill Hall at Oundle where Nikolaus Skoropei went on the night of the murder. (Author's Collection)*

was presented with the hammer and asked to identify it. Unfortunately for the police, none could. He turned to Jack and Joan Peach. They were uncertain. So then he cast his net wider and would have been satisfied to have found anyone who could identify it. Here he had a stroke of luck. Jesse Orders, a woman who had once been engaged to be married to Jack Peach suddenly stepped forward. She had lived with Jack's parents for much of 1946 while he served with the army in Germany. Because of that, she was certain she could make a positive identification and she did, telling police she had remembered it because of the unusually long shaft. According to her statement the hammer had always hung in the coalshed at East Lodge, the house they had lived in until their move the previous year. At that time it had been used as a general-purpose tool rather than just a coal hammer. Irrespective of this, Inspector Tarr was satisfied that provenance had been proven and let the press know that the weapon found was indeed the murder weapon and had probably belonged to the two victims. All he needed next was the man who had wielded it.

By 4 November, three days after the hammer's discovery in the Marsh's vegetable patch, a full inventory of the Peaches' house had also been completed. Other than money, which at that point in the investigation was still proving a contentious issue, the only other thing found to be missing was George Peach's pocket watch. All other possessions had been accounted for. Statements taken from those who had come into contact with George on the day he had been murdered had talked of a pocket watch and at least one man

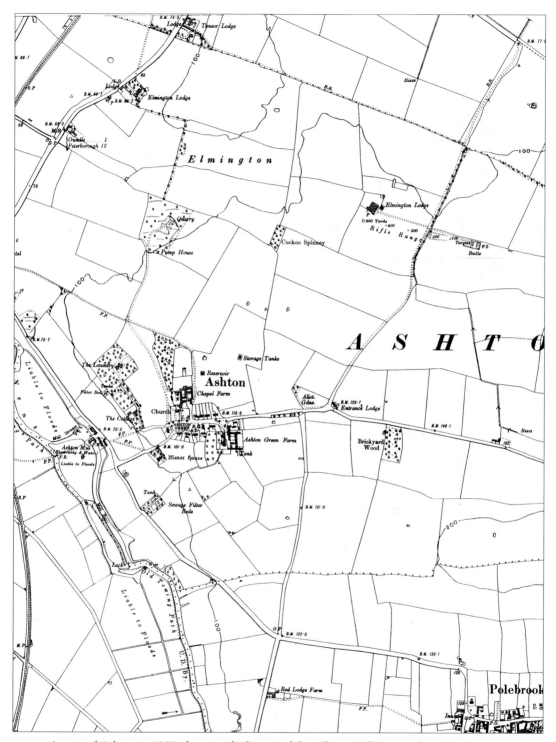

*A map of Ashton in 1927 showing the layout of the village. Mill Farm, where George Peach worked on the day of his murder, is shown beside the Oundle to Polebrook road. West Lodge (or Entrance Lodge) is north of the village centre. (Peterborough Library)*

*The wall behind which the hammer that had been used to kill George and Lillian Peach was found. (Author's Collection)*

had seen it on that Friday afternoon. So they were as near certain as it was possible to be that it had been stolen after the killings. A full description was immediately circulated, but the watch never surfaced.

As the investigation moved into its second week, without any definite leads and no firm suspects, Inspector Tarr began to turn his attentions closer to home. Door-to-door enquiries had unearthed snippets of information that on their own meant nothing, but collectively, however, they told something else. Allegations were being made that indicated all was not well on the estate, or at least on some parts of it. George Peach, it was thought, had information or had uncovered some fact or other that would have brought the world in around someone's ears. Tarr wanted to know who that someone was. Names were mentioned but nothing was ever proven. Just what, if anything, George Peach knew, died with him. Perhaps, said some, that was how it was meant to happen. Tarr never accepted that. Certainly, he had been told through witness statements that the old man had threatened to inform the Hon. Miriam Lane, whose husband, Colonel Lane, managed the estate, of some sort of malpractice involving the cattle, but no evidence ever came to light to substantiate it. As far as he was concerned this was pure speculation, but possibly in his quiet moments he must also have seen a logic to the argument. If it had not been an opportunist theft gone wrong, and murdering George Peach in his sleep had been intentional, then the conspiracy theorists would have been right.

A discovery made on 13 November shifted the emphasis back on to burglary and the entrance made through the narrow pantry window. Twenty

*The picturesque village of Ashton as it was portrayed on postcards in the 1970s. (Author's Collection)*

days after the murders a woman's purse was discovered beneath a hedgerow toward the end of Ashton's main street where the road curved left and dropped away from the houses around the green to its junction with the Oundle to Polebrook road. It lay on top of a bank on the left-hand side of the road some 25 yards away from the gate to Manor Farm, John Dockraye's house. It was of brown leather, flap-over type with a press-stud fastening and thonged leather edges. According to the forensic report it had been out in the open for some time. Just like the hammer, though, it was not easy to prove it had ever belonged to Lillian Peach. Only Jesse Orders, yet again, was clearly certain of its history: 'Mrs Peach had a flap-over purse, light brown leather. I think it was a hand made one. I believe it was made by the blind and it was bound with a darker leather thong binding.'

It was an accurate description as far as the investigating team were concerned and was probably the purse that had been kept upstairs in the handbag, one that no one ever saw because they were not meant to. It was the purse she kept any savings in and occasionally took money from if she bought any treats for herself or items for the house. It was also the purse that had been cast aside by the killer as he made his escape through the village in the early hours of Saturday 25 October, and disappeared into the night.

No other clues were ever forthcoming. Over 2,000 people were eventually fingerprinted by the police team, none of whom ever came near to producing a print that matched the one found on the pantry sill. The broken pantry window pane was never traced. Neither was George Peach's watch, or the key to the back bedroom door, and the hammer's true ownership was never fully established. Inspector Tarr and Detective Sergeant Albert Foster returned to London on 21 January 1953 and the Peach case was placed in the open file of Northampton Police, where it remains to this day.

# INDEX